50 Beaded Bracelets

Step-by-Step Techniques for Beautiful Beadwork Designs

Tammy Honaman

EDITORIAL DIRECTOR: Kerry Bogert

CONTENT EDITORS: Jodi Butler and Hayley DeBerard

ART DIRECTOR & COVER DESIGN: Ashlee Wadeson

INTERIOR DESIGNER: Pamela Uhlenkamp

ILLUSTRATORS: Bonnie Brooks and Laura Shell

PHOTOGRAPHERS: George Boe, Joe Cocoa, Donald Scott, and Ann Swanson

fwcommunity.com

Interweave®

interweave.com

23 22 21 20 19   5 4 3 2 1

SRN: 19BD01
ISBN-13: 978-1-63250-675-7

Contents

Introduction

For more than twenty years, Interweave and *Beadwork* magazine have been inspiring beaders with extraordinary bead weaving patterns. In this gorgeous collection, we've compiled our readers' most-loved bracelet designs. They encompass a wide variety of stitches and styles that you can weave with confidence because each pattern has been carefully selected by a team of dedicated editors who are as passionate about beading as you.

In this carefully curated collection, we included bracelets from *Beadwork* magazine that have received the most attention—designs that our readers liked, shared, and pinned on social media as well as bracelets that beaders took the time to write to us about. We're confident you'll find many bracelet designs that will inspire you to pour beads onto your mat, thread a needle, and dive in.

We can't wait to see which of these stands out as your favorite!

As you thumb through the pages, you'll notice that the book leads you from one bracelet to the next and from one stitch to another so you can make discoveries along the way. There are classic designs made with Japanese seed beads and traditional stitches as well as bracelets that branch out creatively to include multiple types of beads and stitch combinations. This blending of the old and new reflects the breadth of materials and techniques in our bead weaving community today and we're excited to share it with you here.

You'll see bracelets by designers you recognize—from Jill Wiseman to Nichole Starman, Leslee Frumin, and more. All of the contributors share their beautiful bracelets with accessible instructions so you can learn to create amazing jewelry of your own.

Styles include wrap bracelets, cuffs, bangles and everything in-between. Start with your favorite design and see where it leads you.

There are also classic designs, some that are whimsical, and many that will have you dreaming of faraway places. Many artists include variations of their main projects to help as you make substitutions, envision using your favorite colors or interpret a design as a necklace or earrings instead.

There are tips to help guide you along the way and instructions that include how to professionally finish your bracelets.

Clasp styles include manufactured closures and those you weave with beads to match the design. Whether you're new to beading or a seasoned pro, this collection of 50 beloved bracelets is an amazing dose of inspiration and instruction. There are bracelets for purists and renegades alike because everyone has their own style and taste. I've already added a few of these to the top of my to-make list.

Let's get beading!

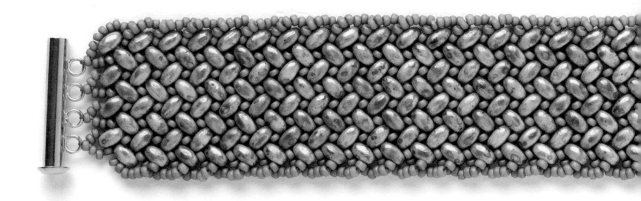

Abbington

Sandie Bachand

techniques
Circular netting variation

Right-angle weave

Ladder stitch

materials
1 g dark green iris size 15° seed beads (A)

1 g olive-green iris size 11° seed beads (B)

24 black 3mm bugle beads (C)

24 matte metallic khaki iris 5mm 2-hole Japanese flat squares (D)

56 gold 4mm crystal pearls (E)

33 red Picasso 4×2.5mm pressed-glass rondelles (F)

6 red 6mm wood rounds (G)

1 gold 9mm round filigree box clasp with 3mm rings

Smoke 6 lb braided beading thread

tools
Size 12 beading needle

Scissors

finished size
7" (18 cm)

① Component 1

Use a variation of circular netting, ladder stitch, and tight tension to form the first diamond-shaped component:

ROUND 1: Use 6' (1.8 m) of thread to string {1D, 1E, 1B, 1E, 1D, 1E, 1F, and 1E} twice, leaving a 6" (15 cm) tail; pass through all the beads again to form a tight circle and tie a square knot with the working and tail threads. Step up through the second (inside) hole of the first D (**FIG. 1, BLUE THREAD**). *NOTE: You will now begin stitching in the opposite direction.*

ROUND 2: String 1F and pass through the second (inside) hole of the next D in Round 1; repeat three times (**FIG. 1, RED THREAD**).

ROUND 3: String 1A, 1C, and 1A; pass through the same hole of the last D exited and the next F in Round 2. *String 1A, 1C, and 1A; pass back through the inside hole of the next D in Round 2.

Pass through the 1A/1C/1A just added and the next F of Round 2. Repeat from * twice (**FIG. 2, PURPLE THREAD**). Pass through the 1A/1C/1A units and adjacent F to tighten the round (**FIG. 2, RED THREAD**). Weave through beads to exit 1F of Round 2 adjacent to 1F of Round 1.

CENTER: String 1B, 1G, and 1B; pass through the F on the opposite side of Round 2. String 1B; pass back through the last G added. String 1B; pass through the first F exited in this round (**FIG. 3, BLUE THREAD**). Weave through beads to exit from the nearest F of Round 1 (**FIG. 3, RED THREAD**).

② Clasp Box

String 1E, 1B, 1E, 1F, 1E, 1B, and 1E; pass through the last F exited and weave through beads to exit from the F just added (**FIG. 4, BLUE THREAD**). String 2B, the box

half of the clasp, and 2B; pass through the last F exited (**FIG. 4, RED THREAD**). Repeat the entire thread path to reinforce. Weave through beads to exit from the F on the opposite side of Round 2 in Component 1.

③ Component 2

Stitch the second component off of the first one:

ROUND 1: Turn the work so the thread exits from the right. String 1E, 1D, 1E, 1B, 1E, 1D, 1E, 1F, 1E, 1D, 1E, 1B, 1E, 1D, and 1E; pass through the last F exited from Component 1 (**FIG. 5, BLUE THREAD**). Pass through the next E and D and step up through the second (inside) hole of the first D added (**FIG. 5, RED THREAD**).

ROUNDS 2–3 AND CENTER: Repeat Rounds 2 and 3 and the center of Component 1. Weave through beads to exit from the F added in Round 1.

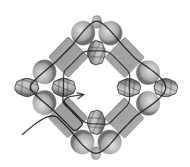

FIG. 1: Forming Rounds 1 and 2 of Component 1

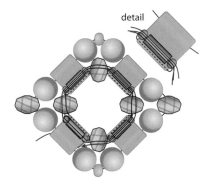

FIG. 2: Adding and tightening Round 3 of Component 1

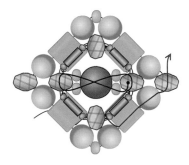

FIG. 3: Stitching the center of Component 1

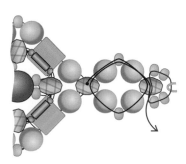

FIG. 4: Adding the box half of the clasp

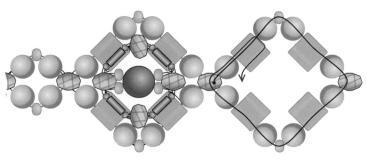

FIG. 5: Forming Round 1 of Component 2

④ Components 3–6

Repeat Component 2 four times or to the desired length, minus ⅝" (1.6 cm) for the clasp.

⑤ Clasp Tab

Repeat Step 2, adding the tab half of the clasp. *NOTE: Take care that the tab is added so it fits into the box properly.* Secure the thread and trim.

Artist's Tips

- Achieve different looks with this design by trying other types of beads, such as pearls, round crystals, and gemstones.

- Use a single component to form a handsome earring: hang a crystal drop from the bottom rondelle and attach a loop and ear wire to the top one.

- Some two-hole flat squares have a "front" and "back." Keep this in mind when stringing these beads, so the visible surfaces are consistent in your design.

- String identical beads between each two-hole flat square, turn the work a quarter turn, and the diamond-shaped component becomes square.

ALTERNATE COLORWAY

MAIN COLORWAY

variation

As showcased in the sparkling blue variation, this pattern also works well using thicker 6mm two-hole CzechMate Tiles in place of the 5mm two-hole Tila flat squares.

Art Deco

Smadar Grossman

techniques

- Right-angle weave
- Fringe
- Netting variation
- Flat herringbone stitch

materials

- 1 g dark silver size 11° Japanese seed beads (A)
- 9 g dark silver size 8° Japanese seed beads (B)
- 2 g dark silver size 6° Japanese seed beads (C)
- 14 topaz 2.5mm crystal bicones (D)
- 12 topaz 4mm crystal bicones (E)
- 6 Pacific opal 4mm crystal bicones (F)
- 6 smoky topaz 6×9mm faceted pressed-glass teardrops (G)
- 4 Pacific opal 8mm fire-polished rounds (H)
- 6 antiqued silver–plated 6mm jump rings
- 1 antiqued silver–plated 13×26mm 3-strand ball-end tube slide clasp
- Smoke 6 lb braided beading thread

tools

- Scissors
- Size 10 and 12 beading needles
- 2 pairs of chain- or flat-nose pliers

finished size

7¾" (19.5 cm)

1 Midline

Use 5' (1.5 m) of thread and a size 10 needle to string {1H, 1A, 1C, and 1A} twice, leaving a 6" (15 cm) tail. Pass through the beads again to reinforce and exit from the first H strung. String 1A, 1C, 1A, 1H, 1A, 1C, and 1A, then pass through the last H exited from the previous unit and continue through the first 1A/1C/1A/1H just added; repeat (**FIG. 1**).

2 Fringe

Work fringes off the midline, then connect them:

FRINGE 1: Use light tension to string 1B, 1E, 1C, 1G (small end first), and 1B; pass back through the 1G/1C just strung. String 1E and 1B; pass through the next 1H/1A/1C/1A/1H of the midline, checking that the fringe just formed is centered between the 2E (**FIG. 2, GREEN THREAD**). *NOTE: Make sure the E of this and the following fringes sit adjacent to the 1A/1C/1A of the midline.*

FRINGE 2: String 1B, 1E, 1C, 1G (small end first), and 1B; pass back through the 1G/1C just added. String 1E; pass back through the nearest B of Fringe 1. Weave through beads to exit up through the first B added in this fringe (**FIG. 2, BLUE THREAD**).

FRINGE 3: String 1E, 1C, 1G, and 1B; pass back through the 1G/1C just added. String 1E and 1B; pass through the final H of the midline (**FIG. 2, RED THREAD**).

FRINGES 4–6: Rotate the work 180 degrees and repeat Fringes 1–3 on the other side of the midline. Switch to a size 12 needle and repeat the thread path of Fringes 1–6 to reinforce. Weave through beads to exit from the tip B of Fringe 1, toward the beadwork. Rotate the work again so Fringes 1–3 point up.

CONNECTIONS: *String 1A, 1C, and 1A and pass through the tip B of the next fringe; repeat. String 1A; pass back through the last B exited.** Weave through the beads of Fringes 3 and 4 to exit from the tip B of Fringe 4, away from the beadwork. String 1A; pass back through the last B exited (**FIG. 3, BLUE THREAD**). Repeat from * to **. Weave through the beads of Fringes 6 and 1 to exit from the tip B of Fringe 1, away from the beadwork. String 1A; pass back through the last B exited and the first 1A/1C added in this section (**FIG. 3, RED THREAD**).

3 Embellish

Embellish the fringe:

STITCH 1: String 1B, 2A, 1B, and 2A; pass through the nearest 1C/1E/1B of Fringe 2 and weave through beads to exit from the mirror C of Fringe 5 (**FIG. 4, GREEN THREAD**).

STITCH 2: String 2A, 1B, 2A, and 1B; pass through the nearest C of the Step 2 fringe connection and back through the last 1B/2A/1B just added. String 2A; pass back through the C of Fringe 6, then weave through beads to exit from the C of Fringe 1. String 2A; pass back through the first 1B/2A/1B added in Stitch 1, then pass through the nearest 1C/1A/1B/1A/1C of the Step 2 fringe connection (**FIG. 4, BLUE THREAD**).

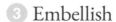

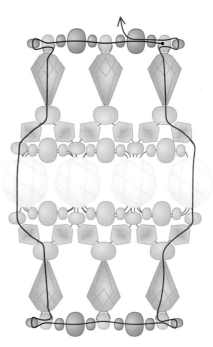

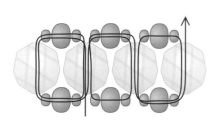

FIG. 1: Forming the midline

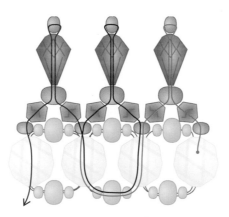

FIG. 2: Adding Fringes 1–3

FIG. 3: Connecting the fringe tips

STITCHES 3 AND 4: Repeat Stitches 1 and 2 to embellish the spaces between Fringes 2 and 3 and between Fringes 4 and 5. Exit through the tip B of Fringe 3, toward the beadwork (**FIG. 4, RED THREAD**).

4 Bands

Combine flat herringbone stitch and a variation of netting to form one side of the bracelet's band:

ROW 1: String 2B, pass through the last B exited, and continue through the nearest 1A/1C/1A/1B; repeat. String 2B; pass through the last B exited and the first B just added (**FIG. 5, BLUE THREAD**).

ROW 2: String 2B, pass down through the next B of Row 1, through the nearest C, and up through the following B of Row 1; repeat. String 2B; pass down through the next B of Row 1 and up through the previous B of Row 1 and the last B added (**FIG. 5, RED THREAD**).

Artist's Tip

- For added sparkle, use crystal rounds (Swarovski article #5000) for H and crystal drop beads (Swarovski article #5500) for G.

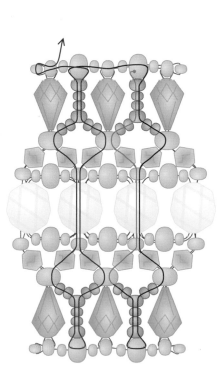

FIG. 4: Embellishing the fringe

FIG. 5: Stitching Rows 1 and 2 of the band

MAIN COLORWAY

ROWS 3 AND 4: String 1F and 2B, pass back through the 1F just added and down through the next B of Row 2, then string 1D, and pass up through the following B of Row 2; repeat. String 1F and 2B; pass back through the F just added, down through the next B of Row 2, up through the previous B of Row 2, through the F just added, and up through the last B added (the outside B) (**FIG. 6**).

ROW 5: String 2B and pass down through the next B of Row 4. String 3A and pass down through the nearest B of Row 2, back through the following D, and up through the next B. String 1A; pass back through the second of the last 3A added. String 1A and pass up through the next B of Row 4 (**FIG. 7, BLUE THREAD**). Repeat from the beginning of this row. String 2A; pass down through the next B of Row 4 and weave through beads to exit up through the last B added (**FIG. 7, RED THREAD**).

ROW 6: String 2B, pass down through the next B of Row 5, then string 1D, and pass up through the following B of Row 5; repeat. String 2B; pass down through the next B of Row 5. To work a turnaround for this and subsequent rows, pass up through the previous B of the previous row and the last B added (**FIG. 8, PURPLE THREAD**).

ROW 7: String 2B, pass down through the next B of Rows 6 and 5, back through the nearest D of Row 5, and up through the next B of Rows 5 and 6; repeat. String 2B, pass down through the next B of Row 5, and work a turnaround (**FIG. 8, GREEN THREAD**).

ROW 8: String 2B and pass down through the next B of Row 7 and the next B of Row 6, then string 1A and pass up through the following B of Rows 6 and 7; repeat. String 2B; pass down through the next B of Row 7 and work a turnaround (**FIG. 8, BLUE THREAD**).

ROW 9: Work 3 herringbone stitches with 2B in each stitch, keeping the thread tight. Work a turnaround (**FIG. 8, RED THREAD**).

ROWS 10–25: Repeat Row 9 sixteen times.

ROWS 26 AND 27: String 1D and 2B; pass back through the D just strung, down through the next B of Row 25, and up through the following B (**FIG. 9, PURPLE THREAD**). String 1A; pass down through the previous B of Row 25 and up through the next B (**FIG. 9, GREEN THREAD**). Repeat from the beginning of this section (**FIG. 9, BLUE THREAD**). String 1D and 2B; pass back through the D just strung, down through the end B of Row 25, then weave through beads to exit up through the last B added (**FIG. 9, RED THREAD**). *NOTE: The D and A make up Row 26; the B make up Row 27.*

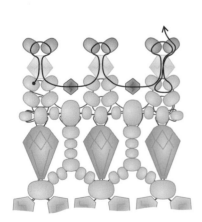

FIG. 6: Adding Rows 3 and 4 of the band

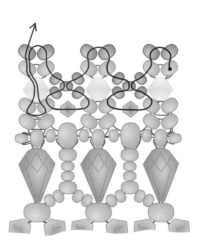

FIG. 7: Forming Row 5 of the band

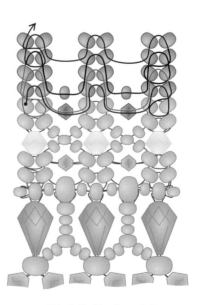

FIG. 8: Working Rows 6–9 of the band

ROW 28 (CLASP LOOPS): String 5A, pass down through the next B of Row 27, through the nearest A of Row 26, and up through the following B of Row 27; repeat. String 5A; pass down through the final B of Row 27, then weave through beads to exit up through the last B added in Row 27 (**FIG. 10**). Repeat the thread path to reinforce. Secure the thread and trim.

Start 6' (1.8 m) of new thread that exits from the tip B of Fringe 4, toward the beadwork. Repeat Rows 1–28 to complete the other bracelet band.

⑤ Clasp

Use 1 jump ring to attach the top loop of one half of the clasp to the top loop on one end of the band; repeat twice using the middle and bottom loops. Repeat this step on the other end of the bracelet using the other half of the clasp and making sure the clasp is positioned to close properly.

variations

- Make a wider version of the bracelet by forming the midline with five right-angle-weave units. Increase the number of fringes, nets, and herringbone stitches accordingly.

- Make a longer bracelet by adding more herringbone rows after Row 25, but finish the band by stitching Rows 26–28.

ALTERNATE COLORWAY

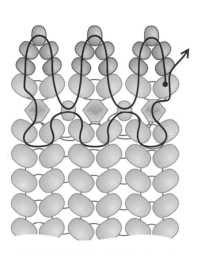

FIG. 9: Adding Rows 26 and 27 of the band

FIG. 10: Adding Row 28 (clasp loops) of the band

Bugle Call

Janice Chatham

techniques

Two-needle right-angle weave

Flat peyote stitch

Fringe

materials

0.5 g metallic dark blue iris size 15° Japanese
seed beads (A)

16 metallic gold size 15° Japanese seed beads (B)

3 g gilded periwinkle size 11° Japanese seed
beads (C)

34 copper size 11° Japanese seed beads (D)

1 g metallic gold size 8° Japanese seed beads (E)

1 g metallic blue iris size 1 (3mm) Japanese
bugle beads (F)

17 mustard yellow Picasso 6mm fire-polished
rounds (G)

1 silver-plated 6×7mm magnetic clasp

2 silver-plated 4mm jump rings

Smoke 6 lb braided beading thread

tools

Scissors

2 size 12 beading needles

2 pairs of chain- or flat-nose pliers

finished size

6¾" (17 cm)

① Clasp Loop 1

Place 1 needle at each end of 6' (1.8 m) of thread. Use the left needle to string 8C to the center of the thread (**FIG. 1, PURPLE THREAD**). Use the right needle to pass back through the last C added to form a loop (**FIG. 1, GREEN THREAD**). *NOTE: Because of the nature of two-needle right-angle weave, the needle will switch left and right positions with each stitch.*

② Base

Use a variation of two-needle right-angle weave and loose tension to form the base row of the bracelet:

UNIT 1: Use the left needle to string 3C and 1G (**FIG. 1, BLUE THREAD**). Use the right needle to string 3C; pass back through the G to form a unit (**FIG. 1, RED THREAD**).

UNIT 2: Use the left needle to string 5C and 1G (**FIG. 2, BLUE THREAD**). Use the right needle to string 5C; pass back through the G to add the next unit (**FIG. 2, RED THREAD**).

UNITS 3–17: Repeat Unit 2 fifteen times.

UNIT 18: Use the left needle to string 4C (**FIG. 3, PURPLE THREAD**). Use the right needle to string 3C; pass back through the last C added on the left side (**FIG. 3, GREEN THREAD**).

③ Clasp Loop 2

Use the left needle to string 7C (**FIG. 3, BLUE THREAD**). Use the right needle to pass back through the 7C just added (**FIG. 3, RED THREAD**). Use each needle to weave through beads, exiting back through the first C added on each needle in Unit 18 of the base. *NOTE: Stitching direction changes at the end of each row, so the right needle is now at the top edge of the base.*

④ Edges

Peyote-stitch along the edges of the base, then add fringes:

TOP EDGE, ROW 1: *Use the right (top) needle to string 1D and pass back through the following C along the edge of the base. String 1C, skip 1C on the edge of the base, and pass back through the following C; repeat. Repeat from * fifteen times. String 1D and pass back through the next C along the edge of the base (**FIG. 4, BLACK THREAD**).

BOTTOM EDGE, ROW 1: Repeat Top edge, Row 1, using the left (bottom) needle. Weave through beads to exit the last C added in Row 1 of the top edge, toward the work (**FIG. 4, PURPLE THREAD**). Use the other needle to weave through beads to exit the last C added in Row 1 of the bottom edge (**FIG. 4, GREEN THREAD**).

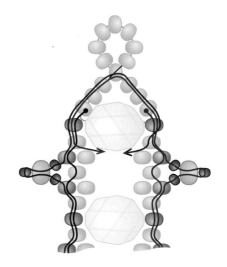

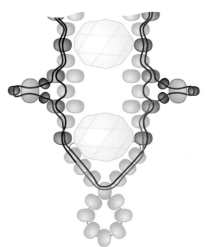

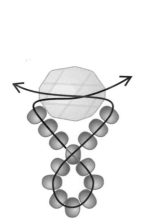

FIG. 1: Forming the first clasp loop and Unit 1 of the base

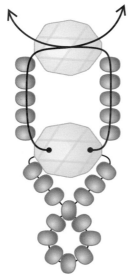

FIG. 2: Stitching Unit 2 of the base

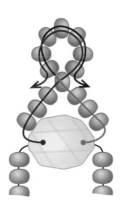

FIG. 3: Working Unit 18 of the base and the second clasp loop

FIG. 4: Adding Row 1 and fringe to the edges

TOP EDGE, FRINGE: **Use the left (top) needle to string 1A, 1E, and 1A; pass back through the E. String 1A and pass back through the following C of the previous row. Weave through beads to exit the next C of the previous row. Repeat from ** fifteen times for a total of 16 fringes. Weave through beads to exit the nearest D/C on the opposite edge of the bracelet, toward the work (**FIG. 4, BLUE THREAD**).

BOTTOM EDGE, FRINGE: Repeat Top edge, fringe, using the right (bottom) needle (**FIG. 4, RED THREAD**).

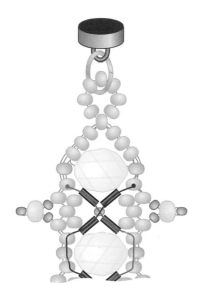

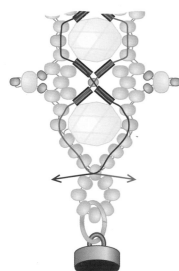

FIG. 5: Stitching the bugle embellishment to the base

⑤ Embellishment

Add bugles and seed beads between the fire-polished rounds to embellish the base:

ROW 1: *Use the right (top) needle to string 1F, 1B, and 1F. Cross the base and pass back through the first C of the same unit on the other side of the base, through the next D, and back through the following C. Use the same needle to repeat from * fifteen times. Weave through beads to exit the last C of Clasp Loop 1 (**FIG. 5, GREEN THREAD**). Secure the thread and trim.

ROW 2: **Use the left (bottom) needle to string 1F; pass through the nearest B in Row 1 of the embellishment. String 1F; pass back through the first C of the same unit on the other side of the base, through the next D, and back through the following C. Use the same needle to repeat from ** fifteen times across the bracelet. Weave through beads to exit the first C of Clasp Loop 1 (**FIG. 5, RED THREAD**). Secure the thread and trim.

⑥ Clasp

Use 1 jump ring to attach 1 clasp loop to one half of the clasp; repeat using the other clasp loop and the other half of the clasp.

Artist's Tips

- Use loose tension on the base row of the bracelet to leave room to add embellishments later.

- For a different look, use only one color of size 15° seed beads.

MAIN COLORWAY

Infinity

Jill Wiseman

techniques

Flat and cubic right-angle weave

Tubular peyote stitch

Picot

materials

15 g metallic gold size 11° seed beads (A)

190 crystal metallic light gold 2×3mm
crystal bicones (B)

2 silver 6mm sew-on snap sets

Smoke 6 lb braided beading thread

tools

Scissors

Size 11 beading needles

finished size

7½" (19 cm) (stretches to 8" [20.5 cm])

① Rings

Form a cubic right-angle-weave ring:

CUBE 1: Use 6' (1.8 m) of thread to string 4A, leaving a 6" (15 cm) tail. Tie the working and tail threads together to form a tight circle. Pass through the first 2A strung to form the first face of the cube. String 3A, pass through the last A exited, and continue through the first 2A just added to form the second face; repeat to form the third face (**FIG. 1, BLUE THREAD**). String 1A; pass through the end A of the first face. String 1A; pass through the last A exited in the third face and the first A added in this fourth face (**FIG. 1, RED THREAD**). Weave through beads to pass through the bottom 4A and the top 4A of the cube to reinforce, exiting from a top A.

CUBE 2, FACE 1: String 3A; pass through the last A exited on the previous cube and the first A just added (**FIG. 2, PURPLE THREAD**).

CUBE 2, FACE 2: String 2A; pass back through the next top A of the previous cube and up through the nearest side A of Cube 2, Face 1. Pass through the 2A just added and the next top A of the previous cube (**FIG. 2, PINK THREAD**).

CUBE 2, FACE 3: String 2A; pass down through the nearest side A of Cube 2, Face 2. Pass through the last A exited at the top of the previous cube and up through the first A just added (**FIG. 2, GREEN THREAD**).

CUBE 2, FACE 4: String 1A; pass down through the nearest side A of Cube 2, Face 1. Pass back through the next top A of the previous cube. Pass up through the nearest side A of Cube 2, Face 3, and through the A just added (**FIG. 2, BLUE THREAD**).

CUBE 2, TOP: Pass through the top 4A of Faces 1–4 in the current cube to reinforce the top of the cube (**FIG. 2, RED THREAD**).

CUBES 3–40: Repeat Cube 2 thirty-eight times.

CUBE 41: Repeat Cube 2, but use the bottom 4A of Cube 1 as the top 4A of this cube (**FIG. 3**) to form a ring. Secure the thread and trim; set the ring aside.

Repeat this entire step six times for a total of 7 rings.

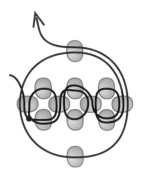

FIG. 1: Forming Cube 1

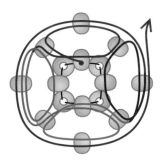

FIG. 2: Stitching Cube 2

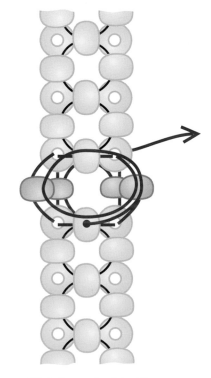

FIG. 3: Connecting Cube 40 to Cube 1 to form a ring

② Center Bands

Stitch a right-angle-weave band and connect it around the center of a ring to form a figure-8 shape:

UNIT 1: String {1B and 1A} twice, leaving a 3" (7.5 cm) tail; pass through all the beads again, then tie a knot with the working and tail threads to form a tight circle. Pass through the first 1B/1A/1B strung to hide the knot (**FIG. 4, GREEN THREAD**).

UNIT 2: String 1A, 1B, and 1A; pass through the last B exited and the first 1A/1B just added (**FIG. 4, BLUE THREAD**); repeat the thread path to reinforce and tighten.

UNITS 3–9: Repeat Unit 2 seven times for a total of 9 units (**FIG. 4, RED THREAD**).

FIG. 4: Forming Units 1–9 of the center band

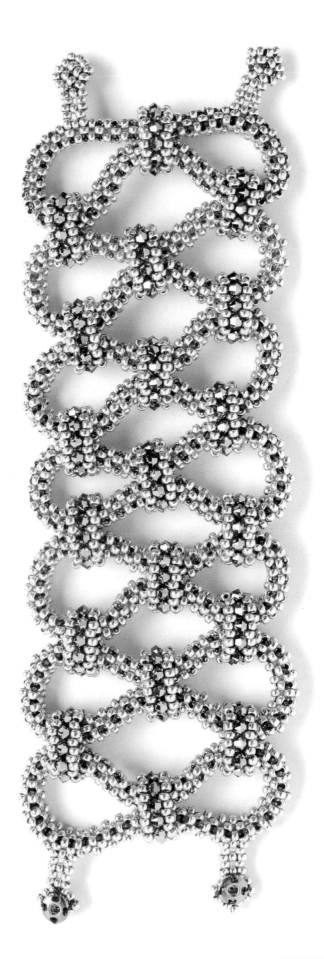

UNIT 10: Fold 1 ring from Step 1 in half and wrap the band around the center. String 1A and pass through the end B of Unit 1, then string 1A and pass through the end B of Unit 9; repeat the thread path to reinforce, tightening the band around the ring. Exit from 1A (**FIG. 5**).

EDGING: String 1A and pass through the next A along the edge of the band; repeat nine times around the band's edge. Weave through beads to exit from 1A at the other edge of the band (**FIG. 6, BLUE THREAD**). Repeat from the beginning of this section to finish the other edge of the band (**FIG. 6, RED THREAD**). Secure the thread and trim. Set the figure-8–shaped component aside.

Repeat this entire step six times to add 1 band around each ring from Step 1.

③ Connecting Bands

Lay 2 components next to one another. Repeat Step 2 to connect the 2 components where they touch at the top, then repeat again to connect them at the bottom. Continue connecting the components in the same manner until all 7 are connected in a line (**FIG. 7**).

④ Clasp Tabs

Right-angle-weave a base for the snaps, forming a clasp tab:

STRIP: Start 4' (1.2 m) of new thread that exits from the upper-left side of 1 end component, directly across from the nearest connecting band. Use A to right-angle-weave a strip 5 units long. Exit from the top A of the fourth unit just formed (**FIG. 8, GREEN THREAD**).

SIDES: String 3A; pass through the last A exited and the next 2A of the strip's fourth unit to exit from the bottom A. String 3A; pass through the last A exited and the 3A just added (**FIG. 8, BLUE THREAD**).

EMBELLISHMENT: String 1A and pass through the next bottom 1A of the next unit; repeat twice. Weave through beads to exit from the top A of the strip's first unit. String 1A and pass through the following top A of the next unit; repeat twice. Pass through all the edge beads at the top of the strip and exit from the bottom A of the strip's fourth unit (**FIG. 8, RED THREAD**).

SNAP: Securely stitch one half of 1 snap to the center of the strip's fourth unit. Secure the thread and trim.

Repeat this entire step on the bottom-left side of the same figure 8, taking care that the snap is on the same side as the previous clasp tab, then repeat the entire step on the other end of the bracelet, taking care that the snaps are placed so they connect properly with the first set of snaps.

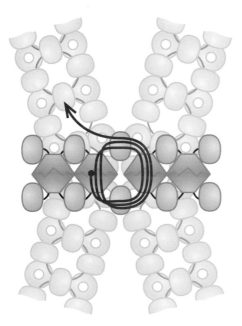

FIG. 5: Completing Unit 10 of the center band while capturing the ring

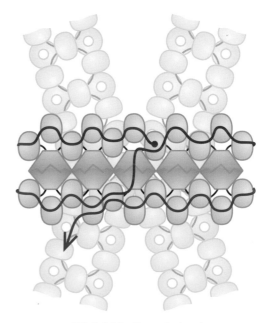

FIG. 6: Edging the center band

FIG. 7: Placing the connecting bands
to join the components

FIG. 8: Stitching the clasp tab

Artist's Tip

• Because the figure-8-shaped
  components stretch, this design
  can fit a variety of wrist sizes.

Pick Up Sticks

Jill Wiseman

techniques

Cubic right-angle weave

Peyote stitch

Stringing

Crimping

materials

20 g metallic nickel size 11° seed beads (A)

2 g metallic nickel size 8° seed beads (B)

38 Montana blue AB 2×3mm crystal bicones (C)

38 aquamarine AB 3mm crystal bicones (D)

49 padparadscha AB 3mm crystal bicones (E)

23 crystal AB 3mm crystal bicones (F)

31 bright gold 3mm crystal pearl rounds (G)

33 light gray 3mm crystal pearl rounds (H)

26 midnight-blue 3mm crystal pearl rounds (I)

4 sterling silver 2mm crimp tubes

1 sterling silver 12mm square 2-strand box clasp
with crystal inlay

Smoke 6 lb braided beading thread

18" (45.5 cm) of .019 beading wire

tools

Scissors

Size 11 beading needle

Wire cutters

Crimping pliers

Bead stop

finished size

7½" (19 cm)

1 Bar 1

Stitch an embellished cubic right-angle weave bar, then finish the edges with peyote stitch:

CUBE 1, BOTTOM: Use 4' (1.2 m) of thread to string 4A, leaving an 8" (20.5 cm) tail. Tie the working and tail threads together to form a tight circle. Pass through the first 3A strung (**FIG. 1, BLACK THREAD**).

CUBE 1, FACE 1: String 1A, 1C, and 1A; pass through the last bottom A exited and the first A just added (**FIG. 1, ORANGE THREAD**).

CUBE 1, FACE 2: String 2A; pass back through the next bottom A, up through the nearest side A of Face 1, through the 2A just added, and the next bottom A (**FIG. 1, PURPLE THREAD**).

CUBE 1, FACE 3: String 2A; pass down through the nearest side A of Face 2, through the last bottom A exited, and up through the first A just added (**FIG. 1, GREEN THREAD**).

CUBE 1, FACE 4: String 1A; pass down through the nearest side A of Face 1, back through the next bottom A, up through the nearest side A of Face 3, and through the A just added (**FIG. 1, BLUE THREAD**).

CUBE 1, TOP: Pass through the 4 top beads of the cube faces, exiting from the C (**FIG. 1, RED THREAD**). Pull the thread tight to complete the first cube. *NOTE: The top of this cube is the bottom of the next cube.*

CUBES 2–9: Repeat Cube 1, Faces 1–4 and top, eight times to form a bar 9 cubes long, using the top of the previous cube as the bottom of the new cube and making sure the C align.

CUBE 10: Repeat Cube 1, this time using A in place of C.

FIRST CORNER: Pass through the top 4 beads of Cube 10 (**FIG. 2, BLUE THREAD**). String 1A and pass through the next bead at the top of Cube 10; repeat three times to add 4 corners to the top of Cube 10 (**FIG. 2, RED THREAD**).

BACK EDGES: Weave through beads to exit the side A of Face 3 in Cube 10, toward the work. String 1A and pass through the nearest side A of the next unit along the long edge of the bar; repeat eight times for a total of 9A. Weave through beads to exit the opposite side A of Cube 1, Face 3. String 1A and pass through the nearest side A of the next unit; repeat to add 1A between the side A of each unit along the other long edge of the bar. Secure the working thread and trim. *NOTE: These peyote-stitch beads*

are placed along the edges of the bar opposite the side with the bicones.

SECOND CORNER: Use the tail thread to add 1A to each corner at the bottom of Cube 1 in a similar manner to the corners of Cube 10. Secure the tail thread and trim. Set the bar aside.

2 Bars 2–24

Repeat Step 1 twenty-three times for a total of 24 bars with the following number of cubes; use the colors indicated in place of C and continue to use A for all other stitches: Bar 2 with D and 8 cubes. Bar 3 with E and 14 cubes. Bar 4 with G and 12 cubes. Bar 5 with C and 8 cubes. Bar 6 with H and 14 cubes. Bar 7 with F and 10 cubes. Bar 8 with D and 12 cubes. Bar 9 with E and 8 cubes. Bar 10 with I and 14 cubes. Bar 11 with G and 10 cubes. Bar 12 with D and 8 cubes. Bar 13 with H and 12 cubes. Bar 14 with C and 14 cubes. Bar 15 with E and 12 cubes. Bar 16 with F and 8 cubes. Bar 17 with C and 10 cubes. Bar 18 with D and 14 cubes. Bar 19 with G and 12 cubes. Bar 20 with E and 8 cubes. Bar 21 with I and 14 cubes. Bar 22 with H and 10 cubes. Bar 23 with E and 12 cubes. Bar 24 with F and 8 cubes.

3 Assembly

String the bars to form the bracelet:

WIRES: *Use one 9" (23 cm) piece of wire to string 1 crimp tube and 1 clasp loop; pass back through the tube and crimp. Repeat from * using the second loop of the same clasp half.

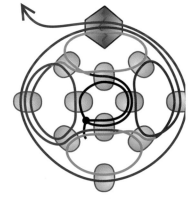

FIG. 1: Forming Cube 1 and the bottom of Cube 2

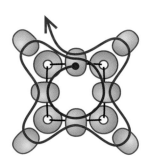

FIG. 2: Adding the corners to the top of Cube 10

BARS: Use each wire to string 1B. Pass 1 wire through the fourth cube of Bar 1; pass the second wire through the seventh cube. Use each wire to string 1B. Pass the top wire through the third cube of Bar 2; pass the bottom wire through the sixth cube, making sure the bicones of Bars 1 and 2 face up (**FIG. 3**). Continue adding 1B to each wire, then stringing the bars in the order in which they were made. *NOTE: Center each bar on the wires, continuing to leave 2 open cubes between wires. Ensure the embellishment bicones and pearls face up.*

CLASP: Place the bead stop on one of the wires. Use the other wire to *string 1B, 1 crimp tube, and the corresponding loop on the other half of the clasp; pass back through the tube and crimp. Remove the bead stop and repeat from *. *NOTE: Take care that the clasp is positioned correctly so that it will close.*

variation

Create a simple necklace by working several bars and stringing them with seed beads onto beading wire.

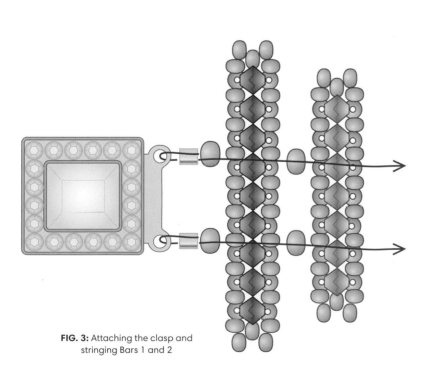

FIG. 3: Attaching the clasp and stringing Bars 1 and 2

Artist's Tips

- When stringing the bars on the beading wire, hold the bracelet up and shake it a little to let the bars settle into place before adding the second half of the clasp. This action will help eliminate any extra beading wire that might show otherwise.

- As you are making and arranging the bars, play with the placement. When you find an arrangement you like, take a photo to ensure that you string them together in the same way.

Tilt-a-Whirl

Penny Dixon

techniques

Flat, circular, and tubular peyote stitch

Netting and circular netting

Fringe

materials

2 g metallic bronze size 15° seed beads (A)

1 g metallic dark blue iris size 15° seed beads (B)

3 g metallic bronze size 11° seed beads (C)

1 g metallic dark blue iris size 11° seed beads (D)

44 dark blue iris 3mm fire-polished rounds (E)

68 bronze 3mm pressed-glass rounds (F)

46 bronze 4mm pressed glass rounds (G)

38 turquoise-and-bronze Picasso 6mm 2-hole flat squares (H)

Smoke 6 lb braided beading thread

tools

Scissors

Size 12 beading needle

finished size

7" (18 cm)

MAIN COLORWAY

① Small Component

Use netting to form the smallest component:

ROUND 1: Use 3' (0.9 m) of thread to string {1G and 2C} six times, leaving a 3" (7.5 cm) tail; tie a knot with the working and tail threads to form a tight circle. Exit through the first 1G/2C (**FIG. 1, BLUE THREAD**).

ROUND 2: String 1A, 1D, and 1A and pass through the next 2C of Round 1; repeat five times, allowing the nets to arc inside the G. Step up through the first 1A/1D added in this round (**FIG. 1, RED THREAD**).

ROUND 3: String 2A and pass through the next 1D of Round 2; repeat five times.

Weave through beads to exit from 1G of Round 1 (**FIG. 2**).

ROUND 4: String 1A, 1H, 1F, 1H, and 1A, then skip 2C/1G of Round 1 and pass through the next 2C/1G; repeat twice to form 3 nets. Step up through the first 1A/1H/1F added in this round (**FIG. 3**).

ROUND 5: Turn the work over so the thread is moving in the opposite direction. String 1F and pass through the next 1F of Round 4; repeat twice. Repeat the thread path to tighten the center circle of F, angling the H so they overlap each other in a pinwheel fashion and sit directly on top of the base. Step up through the first 1F added in this round and the next 1F of Round 4 (**FIG. 4**).

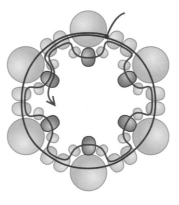

FIG. 1: Forming Rounds 1 and 2 of a small component

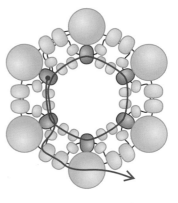

FIG. 2: Finishing Round 3 of a small component

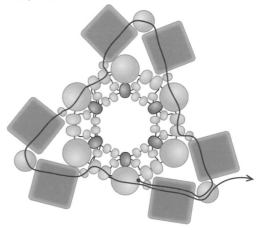

FIG. 3: Adding Round 4 of a small component

ROUND 6: String 3A; pass through the second hole of the nearest 1H. String 2A, 1C, 1E, 1C, and 2A; skip the next 1G/2C of Round 1 and pass through the next 1G of Round 1, 1A of Round 4, the first hole of the nearest 1H, and the nearest 1F (**FIG. 5, BLUE THREAD**). Repeat from the beginning of this round twice. Step up through the next 1F (**FIG. 5, RED THREAD**). Repeat from the beginning of this round to add 3 more nets (**FIG. 6, BLUE THREAD**). Pass through all F again. Secure the tail thread and trim, then weave the working thread through beads to exit from 1G of Round 1 (**FIG. 6, RED THREAD**). Don't trim the thread; set the small component aside. *NOTE: The front half of each new net will sit on top of the previous net.*

Repeat this entire step for a second small component.

② Medium Component

Repeat Step 1 with the following modifications to form a slightly larger component:

ROUND 1: String {2C and 1G} eight times.

ROUND 2: Add a total of 8 nets.

ROUND 3: Use 2B between the 1D, working the sequence eight times.

ROUND 4: Add a total of 4 nets.

ROUND 5: Add a total of 4F.

ROUND 6: Work a total of 8 nets.

Repeat this entire step for a second medium component.

③ Large Component

Repeat Step 1 with the following modifications to form the largest component:

ROUND 1: Use 3½' (1.1 m) of thread to string {2C and 1G} ten times.

ROUND 2: Add a total of 10 nets.

ROUND 3: Use 2B between the 1D, working the sequence ten times.

ROUND 4: Add a total of 5 nets.

ROUND 5: Add a total of 5F.

ROUND 6: Work a total of 10 nets.

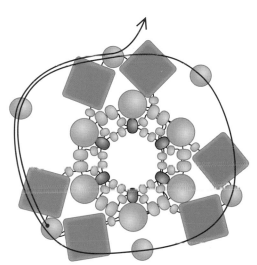

FIG. 4: Stitching Round 5 of the small component

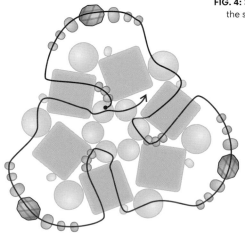

FIG. 5: Adding the first pass of Round 6

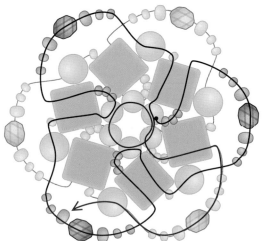

FIG. 6: Stitching the second pass of Round 6

④ Links

Connect the components and embellish the connection:

LINK: Turn 1 small component facedown and use the working thread to string 1F, 1G, and 1F; pass through 1G of 1 medium component and continue through the nearest 1A/1D/2C/1D/1A/1G. String 1F, 1G, and 1F; pass through the mirror 1G/1A/1D/2A/1D/1A/1G of the initial small component and exit from the first 1F added in this round (**FIG. 7, BLUE THREAD**).

EMBELLISH: String 1C, 1E, and 1C; pass back through the third 1F of the link. String 1A; pass through the nearest 2C of Round 1 on the medium component. String 1A; pass back through the second 1F of the link. String 1C; pass back through the 1E just added. String 1C; pass through the fourth 1F of the link. String 1A; pass through the nearest 2C of Round 1 on the small component. String 1A; pass through the first 1F/1G/1F of the link and the nearest 1G of the medium component. Manipulate all the beads and use tight tension to guide the embellishment to sit on the front of the work (**FIG. 7, RED THREAD**). Secure all the threads and trim.

Repeat this entire step three times to connect all the components in a line in this order: small, medium, large, medium, and small.

⑤ Clasp Loop

Form the clasp's loop:

LINK: Start 3' (0.9 m) of new thread that exits from 1G at one end of the bracelet. String {1C and 1F} three times. String 1C; pass through the next 1G at the end of the bracelet and weave through beads to exit from the first 1C just added (**FIG. 8, BLUE THREAD**). String 2A, 1D, and 2A; pass back through the third 1C, second 1F, and second 1C just added. String 2A; pass back through the 1D just added. String 2A; pass through the fourth 1C just added. String 1A; pass through the nearest 2C at the end of the bracelet. String 1A; pass through the first 1C/1F/1C/1F added in this section (**FIG. 8, RED THREAD**).

LOOP, ROUNDS 1 AND 2: String 3C. String {2D and 2C} four times. String 2D and 1C; pass through the last 1F exited and the first 1C just added (**FIG. 9, PURPLE THREAD**).

LOOP, ROUND 3: String 2B, skip 1C, and pass through the next 1C. String 2A, skip 1D, and pass through the next 1D.

Repeat from the beginning of this round four times. Weave through beads to exit from the first 2B added in this round (**FIG. 9, GREEN THREAD**).

LOOP, ROUND 4: Treating the pairs of the previous round as one bead, work 1 stitch with 1D and 1 stitch with 1C; repeat three times. Work 1 stitch with 1D. Weave through beads to exit from the first 1D added in this round (**FIG. 9, BLUE THREAD**).

LOOP, ROUND 5: Work 8 stitches with 1F in each stitch (**FIG. 9, RED THREAD**). Secure the thread and trim. Set the bracelet aside.

⑥ Clasp Bar

Use flat peyote stitch to form a beaded tube and attach it to the bracelet end:

TUBE: Use 16" (40.5 cm) of thread to peyote-stitch a strip 10C wide and 8 rows long. Fold the strip so the first and last rows interlock like a zipper. Weave these beads together to form a seamless tube, and exit through the center of the tube.

END EMBELLISHMENT: String 1E and 1A, then pass back through the 1E and the tube; repeat to add a fringe to the other end of the tube (**FIG. 10, GREEN THREAD**).

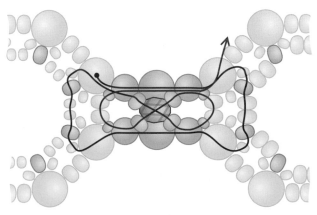

FIG. 7: Connecting the components and embellishing the link

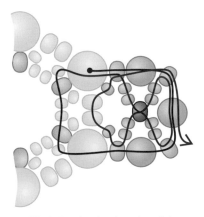

FIG. 8: Forming the clasp-loop link

Repeat the thread path several times to reinforce; secure the thread and trim.

LINK: Repeat the link in Step 5 at the other end of the bracelet, but after completing it, exit from 1C at the end of the link. String 2A and 1C; pass through 4C at the center of the bar and pass back through the 1C just added. String 2A; pass through the other 1C at the end of the link (**FIG. 10, BLUE THREAD**). Weave through beads of the link and repeat the thread path to reinforce (**FIG. 10, RED THREAD**). Secure the thread and trim.

ALTERNATE COLORWAYS

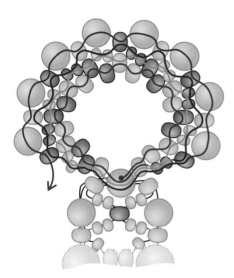

FIG. 9: Stitching the clasp loop

FIG. 10: Finishing the clasp bar and securing it to the link

Artist's Tips

- Tighten the thread after adding each 3-bead net in Round 2 of the component.

- Keep the thread tension tight when working the links and embellishments.

- To preserve the finish of matte beads, buff the piece with Renaissance wax.

- A bit of glue on and around the knots will add extra strength to your piece.

Lilly's Lotus

Gail McLain

technique

Netting

materials

2 g bronze size 15° Japanese seed beads (A)

2 g bronze size 11° Japanese seed beads (B)

86 matte metallic flax 6mm flat 2-hole front-drilled triangles (C)

22 matte metallic flax 6mm 2-hole CzechMates squares (D)

60 amethyst AB 4mm fire-polished rounds (E)

14 amethyst AB 6mm fire-polished rounds (F)

1 gold 16×10mm 2-strand tube clasp

Smoke 6 lb FireLine braided beading thread

tools

Scissors

Size 10 beading needle

finished size

6¾" (17 cm)

① Edges

NOTE: Lay 43 of C on your work surface so that the holes are nearest you and the point of each C is facing away. Add a stop bead to 6' (1.8 cm) of thread, leaving a 12" (30.5 cm) tail. String 1C (left hole/front to back then right hole/back to front), then string 1C (left hole/back to front then right hole/front to back); repeat twenty times (**FIG. 1, BLUE THREAD**). String 1C (left hole/front to back then right hole/back to front) (**FIG. 1, RED THREAD**). Set aside.

Repeat this entire step, this time using 2' (0.6 cm) of thread and leaving a 4" (10 cm) tail, to form a second edge. Remove the needle and add a stop bead to the working thread of the second edge.

② Center Base

Use netting to connect the edges:
Lay the edges horizontally on your work surface with the points of the triangles upright so that each edge mirrors the other, with the first edge on top, and with the long sides that have 22 triangles forming the outside edges of the base, according to **FIG. 2**.

PASS 1: Use the working thread of the first edge to string 2B, 1D, and 2B; pass through the mirror C (right hole/inside to outside) of the second edge. Pass back through the current C (left hole/outside to inside) and the nearest C (right hole/outside to inside). String 1B; pass through the unused (second) hole of the last D added. String 1B; pass through the mirror C (right hole/inside to outside) of the first edge, the nearest C (left hole/inside to outside), the next C (right hole/outside to inside) and the following C (left hole/outside to inside) (**FIG. 2, PURPLE THREAD; TOP VIEW OF BEADWORK SHOWN**).

PASS 2: String 1B, 1D, and 1B; pass through the mirror C (left hole/inside to outside) of the second edge, the nearest C (right hole/inside to outside then left hole/outside to inside), and the next C (right hole/outside to inside). String 1B; pass through the unused (second) hole of the last D added. String 1B; pass through the mirror C (right hole/inside to outside) of the first edge, the nearest C (left hole/inside to outside), the next C (right hole/

outside to inside), and the following C (left hole/outside to inside) (**FIG. 2, GREEN THREAD**).

PASS 3–21: Repeat Pass 2 nineteen times (**FIG. 2, BLUE THREAD**).

PASS 22: String 1B, 1D, and 1B; pass through the mirror C (left hole/inside to outside) and the nearest C (right hole/inside to outside then left hole/outside to inside). String 2B; pass through the unused (second) hole of the last D added. String 2B; pass through the mirror C (left hole/inside to outside). Weave through beads to exit from the endmost C (left hole/outside to inside) of the second edge (**FIG. 2, RED THREAD**).

FIG. 1: Stitching the edges

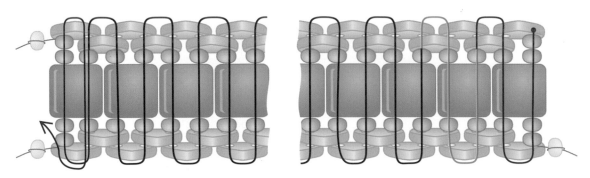

FIG. 2: Forming the center base

Artist's Tips

- Use firm tension to stitch this bracelet. Don't worry if the beadwork seems loose; the more embellishment nets you work, the more the bracelet will tighten up.

- If you are planning to increase or decrease the bracelet length, know that each pair of triangles will adjust the length by ⅜" (1 cm).

ALTERNATE COLORWAYS

③ Center Embellishment

Use netting to embellish the center:

PASS 1: String {1B and 1E} twice, then string 1B; pass through the mirror C (left hole/inside to outside). String 3A; pass back through the current C (right hole/outside to inside) and the nearest C (left hole/outside to inside) (**FIG. 3, BLUE THREAD**).

PASS 2: String 1E, 1B, and 1E; pass through the mirror C (left hole/inside to outside) and the nearest C (right hole/inside to outside). String 3A; pass through the nearest C (left hole/outside to inside) and the next C (right hole/outside to inside). String 1E, 1B, and 1E; pass through the mirror C (right hole/inside to outside) and the nearest C (left hole/inside to outside). String 3A; pass back through the current C (right hole/outside to inside) and the nearest C (left hole/outside to inside) (**FIG. 3, RED THREAD**).

PASSES 3–5: Repeat Pass 2 three times.

PASS 6: String 1B, 1F, and 1B; pass through the mirror C (left hole/inside to outside) and the nearest C (right hole/inside to outside). String 3A; pass through the nearest C (left hole/outside to inside) and the next C (right hole/outside to inside) (**FIG. 4, BLUE THREAD**). String 1E, 1B, and 1E; pass through the mirror C (right hole/inside to outside) and the nearest C (left hole/inside to outside). String 3A; pass back through the current C (right hole/outside to inside) and the nearest C (left hole/outside to inside) (**FIG. 4, RED THREAD**).

PASSES 7–19: Repeat Pass 6 thirteen times.

PASSES 20–22: Repeat Pass 2 three times.

PASS 23: String {1B and 1E} twice, then string 1B; pass through the mirror C (right hole/inside to outside).

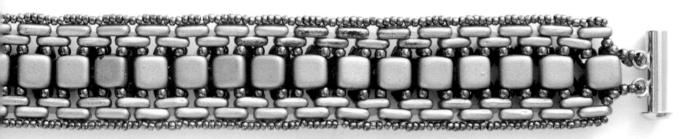

BACK OF BRACELET

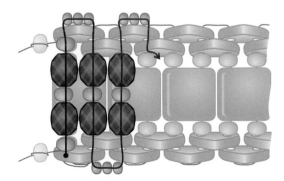

FIG. 3: Working Passes 1 and 2 of the center embellishment

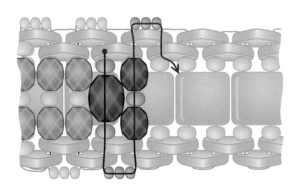

FIG. 4: Adding Pass 6 of the center embellishment

④ Edge Embellishment

String 3A and pass through the next 3A of this edge; repeat twenty times. String 3A; pass through the nearest C (left hole/outside to inside) and weave through beads to exit from the nearest 3A of the opposite edge (**FIG. 5, BLUE THREAD**).

Repeat this entire step to embellish the other edge. Weave through beads to exit from the outside hole of the nearest end D (**FIG. 5, RED THREAD**).

⑤ Clasp

String 1B, 3A, 1 loop of one half of the clasp, and 2A; pass back through the last B added and the last D (outside hole) exited. String 1B, 3A, the second loop of the same half of the clasp, and 2A; pass back through the last B added and the last D (outside hole) exited (**FIG. 6**). Repeat the thread path of this clasp to reinforce. Secure this thread and trim.

Remove the stop bead from the longest tail thread at the other end of the bracelet and use the thread to pass through the outside hole of the nearest end D, then repeat this entire step, using the second half of the clasp and taking care that the clasp is positioned to close properly. Remove the remaining stop beads; secure and trim the threads.

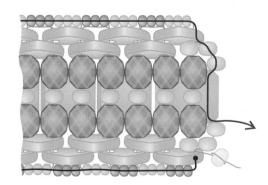

FIG. 5: Forming the edge embellishment

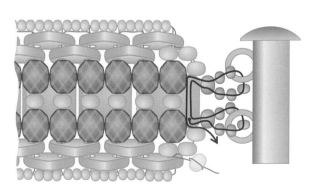

FIG. 6: Attaching the clasp

Raspberry Strata

Rachel Sim

techniques

Flat spiral stitch

Netting

materials

7 g matte metallic dark bronze size 15° seed beads (A)

2 g matte metallic khaki iris size 11° seed beads (B)

10 g raspberry-lined smoky amethyst 3.4mm drops (C)

114 metallic bronze 4mm fire-polished rounds (D)

6 gold 5mm jump rings

1 gold 10×21mm 3-strand tube clasp

Smoke 6 lb braided beading thread

tools

Scissors

Size 10 and 12 beading needles

2 pairs of chain- or flat-nose pliers

finished size

7" (18 cm)

① Strip 1

Work a strip of flat spiral stitch to form one side of the bracelet:

STRIP 1, STITCH 1: Use 7' (2.1 m) of thread to string 2D, 4A, 1C, and 4A, leaving an 8" (20.5 cm) tail; pass through the first 2D to form an arc (**FIG. 1, BLUE THREAD**).

STRIP 1, STITCH 2: String 4A, 1C, and 4A; pass up through the 2D of Stitch 1 to form another arc (**FIG. 1, RED THREAD**). Arrange the beads so that there is 1 arc on each side of the 2D.

STRIP 1, STITCH 3: String 1D, 4A, 1C, and 4A; pass up through the top D of the previous stitch and the D just added. Push this arc to the left (**FIG. 2, BLUE THREAD**). *NOTE: Make sure the beads added in this and each of the following stitches lie on top of the previously added beads.*

STRIP 1, STITCH 4: String 4A, 1C and 4A; pass up through the last 2D exited and push this arc to the right (**FIG. 2, RED THREAD**).

STRIP 1, STITCHES 5–74: Repeat Stitches 3 and 4 thirty-five times for a total of 38D down the center of the strip.

CLASP LOOPS: String 6A and 1 jump ring; pass back through the first A just added and the last 2D of the strip to form a loop (**FIG. 3**). Check that the beads are snug around the jump ring and adjust the number of beads as necessary. Weave through beads to exit up through the final 2D. Repeat the loop thread path to reinforce; secure the thread and trim. Place a needle on the tail thread and add another jump ring to the other end of the strip; secure the thread and trim.

② Strip 2

Repeat Step 1 to make a second strip.

③ Center Strip

Work a third flat spiral-stitch strip, incorporating beads from Strips 1 and 2:

ARRANGE: Place Strips 1 and 2 next to each other with the arcs laying in the same direction and the first stitches at the bottom.

CENTER STITCH 1: Use 10' (3 m) of new thread to string 2D and 3A, leaving a 3' (0.9 cm) tail; pass down through the middle 1A/1C/1A of the first arc to the left. String 3A; pass up through the 2D just added (**FIG. 4, PURPLE THREAD**). *NOTE: Make sure the C of Strips 1 and 2 point up in this and each of the following stitches. Check the drops after each stitch to make sure they are positioned correctly as they can't be straightened afterwards.*

CENTER STITCH 2: Working with very tight tension, string 3A; pass down through the middle 1A/1C/1A of the first arc to the right. String 3A; pass up through the last 2D added (**FIG. 4, GREEN THREAD**).

CENTER STITCH 3: String 1D and 3A; pass down through the middle 1A/1C/1A of the next arc to the left. String 3A; pass up through the top D of the previous stitch and the D just added (**FIG. 4, BLUE THREAD**).

CENTER STITCH 4: String 3A; pass down through the middle 1A/1C/1A of the next arc to the right. String 3A; pass up through the top D of the previous stitch and the D just added (**FIG. 4, RED THREAD**).

Repeat Stitches 3 and 4 thirty-five times to connect Strips 1 and 2.

JUMP RING: Repeat Step 1, clasp loops to add a jump ring to each end of this center strip; secure and trim the working thread, but not the tail thread.

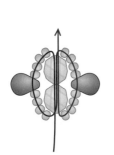

FIG. 1: Forming Stitches 1 and 2 of Strip 1

FIG. 2: Working Stitches 3 and 4 of Strip 1

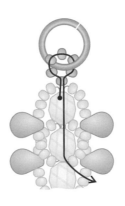

FIG. 3: Attaching a jump ring

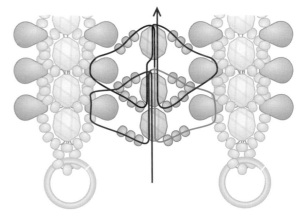

FIG. 4: Connecting the strips

④ Embellishment

Add drops to form a netted ridge on top of the center:

RIGHT SIDE: Weave the tail thread of the center strip through beads to exit from the nearest C on Strip 2 (to the right of center) (**FIG. 5, BLUE THREAD**). String 1B, 1C, and 1B, then pass through the C above the last one exited (**FIG. 5, RED THREAD**); repeat for the length of the strip. Pass through the nearest 4A moving toward the center, the 6A of the center clasp loop, back through the first A of the loop, and the next 4A/1C of the nearest left arc (**FIG. 6, BLUE THREAD**).

LEFT SIDE: Working with tight tension, string 1B and pass back through the last C added on the right side embellishment, then string 1B and pass through the next C of Strip 1 (to the left of center) (**FIG. 6, RED THREAD**); repeat for the length of the bracelet. Secure the thread and trim.

⑤ Clasp

Attach each jump ring to a loop of the clasp, ensuring the clasp will close properly when worn.

Artist's Tips

- When working flat spiral stitch, be mindful to work the overlapping arcs consistently for the whole strip.

- The lengths of the threads in the instructions are calculated so you don't have to add thread while working. If you don't like using long threads, you can work with shorter threads and add thread when needed.

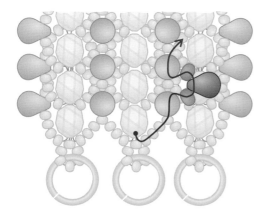

FIG. 5: Embellishing the right side

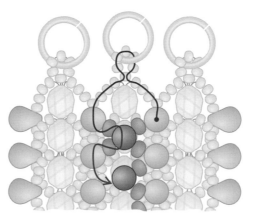

FIG. 6: Embellishing the left side

Lost in the Sahara

Hortense E. Thompson

techniques

2-needle right-angle weave

Peyote stitch variation

materials

4 g metallic bronze size 11° seed beads (A)

4 g silky bronze 5×2.5mm 2-hole SuperDuos (B)

6 sunflower yellow Picasso 6mm 2-hole DiscDuos (C)

12 crystal amber full 10×3mm 3-hole AVA beads (D)

1 amber Picasso 14mm 2-hole cup button

10 bronze 3mm pearl rounds (E)

20 bronze 4mm pearl rounds (F)

Crystal 6 lb FireLine braided beading thread

tools

Scissors

2 size 10 beading needles

finished size

7" (18 cm)

① Base

Use two-needle right-angle weave to stitch the bracelet base:

CLASP BUTTON: Place a needle at each end of 6' (1.8 m) of thread. Use the right needle to string 3A and one hole of the cup button (concave side first) (**FIG. 1, TURQUOISE THREAD**); use the left needle to pass through the second hole in the cup button (**FIG. 1, ORANGE THREAD**). Center the beads on the thread.

END 1: Use the right needle to string 5A, 1B, 3A, and the center hole of 1D (**FIG. 1, PURPLE THREAD**). Use the left needle to string 5A and pass through the second hole of the B, then string 3A and pass back through the center hole of the D (**FIG. 1, GREEN THREAD**). *NOTE: Because of the nature of two-needle right-angle weave, the needles will switch left and right positions with each stitch.*

PASS 1: Use the right needle to string 4A and pass through the end right hole of the D, then string 1C and pass through the end left hole of the D (**FIG. 1, BLUE THREAD**). Use the left needle to string 4A and pass back through the end left hole of the D, the first hole of the C, and the end right hole of the D (**FIG. 1, RED THREAD**).

PASS 2: Use the right needle to string 1B and 3A, then pass back through the second hole of the B; string one end hole of 1D and pass through the second hole of the C and the other end hole of the D just added (**FIG. 2, ORANGE THREAD**). Use the left needle to string 1B and 3A, then pass back through the second hole of the B; pass back through the second end hole of the D added in this pass, the C (second hole), and the first end hole of the D (**FIG. 2, TURQUOISE THREAD**).

PASS 3: Use the right needle to string 4A and pass through the center hole of the D (**FIG. 2, PURPLE THREAD**); repeat using the left needle (**FIG. 2, GREEN THREAD**).

PASS 4: Use the right needle to string {1A and 1B} three times; string 1A and the center hole of 1D (**FIG. 2, BLUE THREAD**). Use the left needle to string {1A and 1B} three times; string 1A and pass back through the center hole of the last D added (**FIG. 2, RED THREAD**).

PASSES 5–23: Repeat Passes 1–4 four times. Repeat Passes 1–3.

END 2: Use the right needle to string 3A and 1B (**FIG. 3, PURPLE THREAD**). Use the left needle to string 3A and pass through the second hole of the B just added (**FIG. 3, GREEN THREAD**).

CLASP LOOP: Use the right needle to string 26A and pass back through the second hole of the B and the nearest 7A (**FIG. 3, BLUE THREAD**); use the left needle to repeat the thread path in reverse to reinforce (**FIG. 3, RED THREAD**). Rotate the beadwork clockwise ninety degrees.

FIG. 1: Adding the clasp button, End 1, and Pass 1 of the base

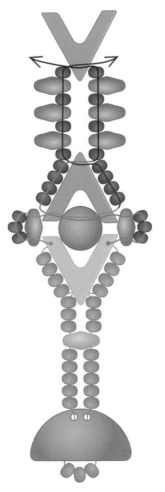

FIG. 2: Forming Passes 2–4 of the base

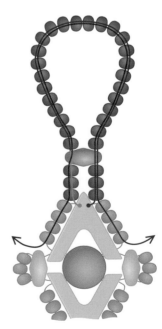

FIG. 3: Finishing End 2 and the clasp loop of the base

2 Edges

Use a variation of peyote stitch to add edges to finish the base:

PASSES 1 AND 2: *NOTE: Work the entire top edge first using the top needle.* Use the top needle to string 2A; pass back through the nearest 3A. String 2A; pass back through the following 3A. String 1A; pass through the second (outside) hole of the next B. String 1B and pass through the next B (outside hole); repeat. String 1A; skip the first A of the next 4A set and pass back through the following 3A (**FIG. 4, TURQUOISE THREAD**). Using the top needle, repeat from the beginning of this pass four times (**FIG. 4, ORANGE THREAD**).

Use the top needle to string 2A and pass back through the nearest 3A, then string 2A and pass back through the following 4A (**FIG. 4, PURPLE THREAD**). Use the bottom needle to repeat from the beginning of this pass along the bottom edge (**FIG. 4, GREEN THREAD**). Use the top needle to weave through beads of the clasp and exit back through the last 2A added with the bottom needle and the next 4A (**FIG. 4, BLUE THREAD**); repeat using the bottom needle (**FIG. 4, RED THREAD**).

PASSES 3 AND 4: *NOTE: Work the entire top edge first using the top needle.* Use the top needle to string 1A, 1F, and 1A; pass through the nearest B (outside hole) of the previous pass. String 1E; pass through the next B (outside hole) of the previous pass. String 1A, 1F, and 1A; skip the first A of the nearest 2A set in the previous pass and pass through the next 5A (**FIG. 5, GREEN THREAD**). Using the top needle, repeat from the beginning of this pass four times (**FIG. 5, BLUE THREAD**). Weave through beads of the clasp to reinforce. Use the bottom needle to repeat from the beginning of this pass along the other edge (**FIG. 5, RED THREAD**). Secure and trim the threads.

Artist's Tip

- The clasp adds about an inch (2.5 cm). Take this into account when determining the number of motifs to make.

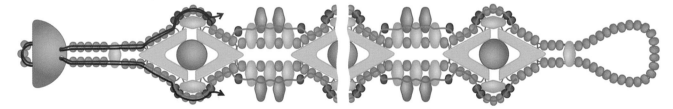

FIG. 4: Stitching Passes 1 and 2 of the edges

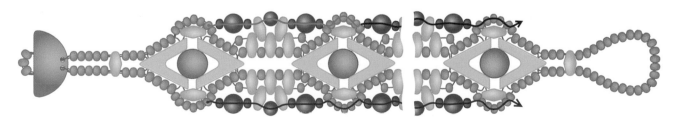

FIG. 5: Forming Passes 3 and 4 of the edges

Lissome Plum

Roxi Rogers

techniques

Ladder stitch

Flat herringbone stitch

Circular peyote stitch

materials

11 g metallic plum size 11° seed beads (A)

5 g marbled opaque pink size 8° seed beads (B)

1 brown 15mm carved floral plastic shank button

Smoke 6 lb braided beading thread

Thread conditioner

tools

Scissors

Size 10 beading needle

finished size

20" (51 cm)

① Band

Use ladder and flat herringbone stitches to form the bracelet band:

ROWS 1 AND 2: Use 6' (1.8 m) of conditioned thread to string 4A, leaving a 12" (30.5 cm) tail. Pass through the beads again to form a tight circle (**FIG. 1, GREEN THREAD**). String 2A, then pass through the previous 2A and the 2A just added (**FIG. 1, BLUE THREAD**); repeat twice for a total of five 2A-high ladder-stitched columns (**FIG 1, RED THREAD**).

ROW 3: String 2A; pass down through the next 2A of Rows 1 and 2 and up through the following A of Row 1 (**FIG. 2, GREEN THREAD**). Skip the nearest A of Row 2 and pass up through the following A of Row 2. String 2A; pass down through the next A of Row 2 (**FIG. 2, BLUE THREAD**). Step up for the next and subsequent rows by weaving through beads to work a turnaround and exit back up through the last A added (**FIG. 2, RED THREAD**). *NOTE: The stitching direction will change with each new row.*

ROW 4: String 2A; pass down through the next A in the previous row (**FIG. 3, GREEN THREAD**). String 1B; skip the next A of the previous row and pass up through the following A (**FIG. 3, BLUE THREAD**). String 2A; pass down through the next A and step up (**FIG. 3, RED THREAD**).

ROW 5: String 2A; pass down through the next A of the previous row, back through the next B, and up through the following A. String 2A; pass down through the next A and step up (**FIG. 4**).

ROWS 6–284: Repeat Rows 4 and 5 seventy times until the band is 19½" (49.5 cm) long or the desired bracelet length minus 1" (2.5 cm) for the clasp.

ROW 285: String 2A; pass down through the next A of the previous row. String 1A; skip the nearest B and pass up through the next A of the previous row. String 2A; pass down through the next A and step up.

Row 286: String 2A; pass down through the next A of the previous row and up through the following A. *NOTE: This will create a decrease in your work.* String 2A; pass down through the next A and step up.

ROW 287: Work 1 row of herringbone stitch with 2A in each stitch.

② Clasp

Use circular peyote stitch to create a clasp loop, then add the button to the other end of the band:

LOOP: String 21A; pass down through the A on the other end of the 2 previous rows. Work a turnaround to exit back up through the last end A (**FIG. 5, GREEN THREAD**). String 1A, skip 1A of the 21A just added, and pass through the following A; repeat nine times for a total of 10A. String 1A and pass through the nearest end 2A of the last herringbone rows. Work a turnaround and step up through the last A added (**FIG. 5, BLUE THREAD**). String 1B and pass through the following A of the previous round; repeat nine times for a total of 10B (**FIG. 5, RED THREAD**). Secure the thread and trim.

BUTTON: Add a needle to the tail thread. String 5A, the button, and 4A; pass down through the 2A on the other end of Rows 1 and 2. Work a turnaround to pass up through the last end A of Row 1 and pass back through all the beads just added and the first end A (**FIG. 6**). Repeat the thread path to reinforce. Secure the thread and trim.

FIG. 1: Forming Rows 1 and 2 of the band

FIG. 2: Using herringbone stitch to add Row 3 to the band

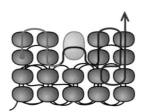

FIG. 3: Adding Row 4 and the first B to the band

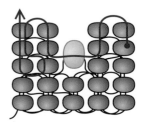

FIG. 4: Working Row 5 of the band

MAIN COLORWAY

ALTERNATE COLORWAY

Artist's Tip

- Keep the tail to the left. You will know when to add the B to a row when you are stitching left to right.

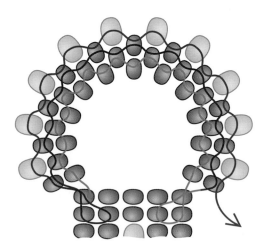

FIG. 5: Stitching the clasp loop

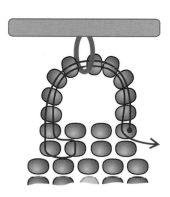

FIG. 6: Adding the button for the clasp

Moroccan Essence

Barbara Falkowitz and Amy Haftkowycz

techniques

Right-angle weave

Stringing

materials

10 g metallic copper size 11° seed beads (A)

28 Caribbean blue opal 3mm crystal bicones (B)

8 turquoise 3mm crystal bicones (C)

40 Caribbean blue opal 4mm crystal bicones (D)

34 Pacific opal 4mm crystal bicones (E)

60 opaque rose topaz 3mm fire-polished rounds (F)

1 antiqued copper 10×26mm 4-strand tube slide clasp

Smoke 6 lb braided beading thread

tools

Scissors

Size 10 or 12 beading needle

finished size

6½" (16.5 cm)

1 Square Component Bases

Use right-angle weave to form square-shaped component bases:

ROW 1, UNIT 1: Use 6' (1.8 m) of thread to string 8A, leaving a 4" (10 cm) tail. Tie a knot with the working and tail threads to form a tight circle; pass through the first 6A (**FIG. 1, ORANGE THREAD**). *NOTE: Work with tight tension, but keep in mind that the embellishments will also help square the units.*

ROW 1, UNIT 2: String 6A; pass through the last 2A exited from the previous unit and the first 4A just added (**FIG. 1, GREEN THREAD**).

ROW 1, UNITS 3–5: Repeat Unit 2 three times (**FIG. 1, BLUE THREAD**).

ROW 1, UNIT 6: String 6A; pass through the last 2A exited from the previous unit and the first 2A just added (**FIG. 1, RED THREAD**).

ROW 2, UNIT 1: String 6A; pass through the last 2A exited from the previous unit, the 6A just added, and the top 2A of the next unit in the previous row (**FIG. 2, ORANGE THREAD**).

ROW 2, UNIT 2: String 4A; pass down through the side 2A of the previous unit, the last 2A exited from the previous row, and up through the first 2A just added (**FIG. 2, GREEN THREAD**).

ROW 2, UNIT 3: String 4A; pass through the top 2A of the next unit in the previous row, up through the side 2A of the previous unit, the 4A just added, and the top 2A of the following unit in the previous row (**FIG. 2, BLUE THREAD**).

ROW 2, UNITS 4–6: Repeat Units 2 and 3 once, then repeat Unit 2, this time exiting from the last 2A added (**FIG. 2, RED THREAD**).

ROWS 3–6: Continue working 6 units in each row for 4 more rows, forming a total of 6 rows. Weave through beads to exit down through 2A at the end of Row 6. Don't trim the thread; set aside.

Repeat this entire step twice for a total of 3 square bases.

2 Rectangle Component Bases

Repeat Step 1, Rows 1 and 2; set aside. Repeat to form a second rectangle base. *NOTE: These will be used for connecting the clasp to the bracelet.*

3 Square Embellishments

Embellish the square component bases:

ROUND 1: Use the working thread of 1 square component base to string 1D; pass down through the next vertical 2A of this row to seat the bicone diagonally across the unit. Repeat to add 1D in the center of Units 5–2 of Row 6, then weave through beads of Unit 1 to exit from the top 2A, toward the work (**FIG. 3, ORANGE THREAD**). Add 1D to each unit down the side of the square as before, turning the corner on the last unit; repeat around each edge. Exit down through the inner 2A of Unit 1, Row 5 (**FIG. 3, GREEN THREAD**).

Artist's Tip

- The base units may seem less than square when you stitch them, but they will tighten up nicely once the embellishment is added.

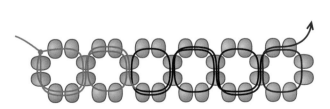

FIG. 1: Forming Row 1 of the base

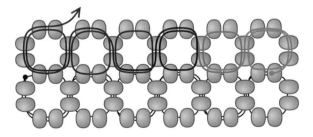

FIG. 2: Stitching Row 2 of the base

ROUND 2: In the same fashion as Round 1, add 1F to each unit that touches the units embellished by D (**FIG. 3, BLUE THREAD**).

ROUND 3: In the same fashion as Round 1, add 1C to each unit that touches the units embellished by F (**FIG. 3, RED THREAD**). Secure the thread and trim. This is a side component. Set aside.

Repeat this entire step to form a second side component. Repeat again, substituting E for D and B for C, to form the center component.

④ **Rectangle Embellishments**

Embellish 1 rectangle base as in Step 3, this time adding 1E to each unit of the first row, then adding 1F to the first 2 units of Row 2, 1B to Units 3 and 4, and 1F to Units 5 and 6 (**FIG. 4**). Secure the thread and trim; set this rectangle component aside. Repeat this step to embellish the remaining rectangle base.

variation

For a pendant, stitch one square with six-by-six units and the two others with four-by-four units. Adjust the connecting strands and finish with filigree and chain as desired.

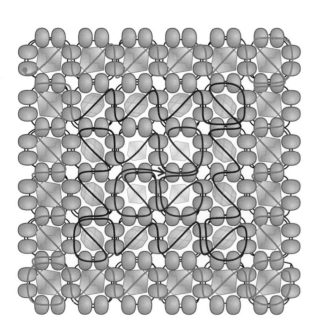

FIG. 3: Embellishing a square component base

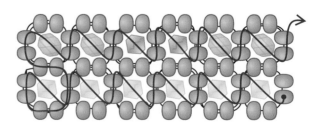

FIG. 4: Embellishing a rectangle component

5 Connection 1

Attach the left side component to the center component:

TOPMOST CONNECTION: Turn 1 side component so it is positioned like a diamond. Start 4' (1.2 m) of new thread that exits up through the end 2A of the second unit from the top point on the right. String 3A, 1F, 5A, 1B, 5A, 1F, and 3A; pass down through the mirror 2A of the center component (**FIG. 5, ORANGE THREAD**). String 3A and pass back through the last F added in this section. String 5A; pass back through the B of this section. String 5A; pass back through the first F added in this section. String 3A; pass up through the first 2A exited in this section. Weave through beads to exit up through the end 2A of the fourth unit from the top point of the side component on the right (**FIG. 5, PURPLE THREAD**).

TOP MIDDLE CONNECTION: String 3A, 1B, 1A, 1F, 1A, 1B, and 3A; pass down through the mirror 2A of the center component. String 3A; pass back through the last 1B/1A/1F/1A/1B added in this section. String 3A; pass up through the first 2A exited in this section. Weave through beads to exit up through the corner 2A on the rightmost corner point of the side component (**FIG. 5, GREEN THREAD**).

CENTER CONNECTION: String 1A, 1E, and 1A; pass down through the mirror 2A of the center component. String 1A; pass back through the E added in this section. String 1A and weave through beads to exit down through the end 2A of the third unit down from the side component's corner point (**FIG. 5, BLUE THREAD**).

BOTTOM CONNECTIONS: Repeat the top middle and topmost connections to form mirror attachments at the bottom of the side and center components. Weave through beads to exit down through the end 2A of the third unit to the left of the side component's bottom point (**FIG. 5, RED THREAD**).

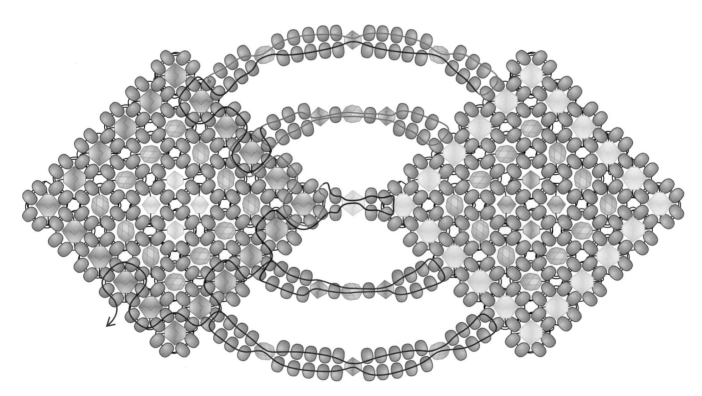

FIG. 5: Connecting the left side and center components

⑥ Connection 2

Connect the left side component to 1 rectangle component:

BOTTOM CONNECTION: Place 1 rectangle component so it sits vertically to the left of the beadwork, with the E-embellished row to the left. String 2A, 1B, 2A, 1B, and 2A; pass up through the side 2A of the bottom unit along the right side of the rectangle component (an F-embellished unit). String 2A; pass back through the next 1B/2A/1B added in this section. String 2A; pass down through the first 2A exited in this section. Weave through beads to exit up through the 2A on the bottom side of the side component's leftmost corner (**FIG. 6, GREEN THREAD**).

CENTER CONNECTIONS: String 1A, 1F, and 1A; pass down through the side 2A of the third unit from the bottom along the right side of the rectangle component. String 1A; pass back through the last F added. String 1A; pass up through the first 2A exited in this section and the next 2A on the corner. Repeat this section to connect to the fourth unit from the bottom of the rectangle component. Weave through beads to exit down through the end 2A of the third unit to the left of the side component's topmost corner (**FIG. 6, BLUE THREAD**).

TOP CONNECTION: Repeat the bottom connection, this time connecting to the top right-side unit of the rectangle component. Weave through beads to exit down through the end 2A of the second unit from the top on the left side of the rectangle component (**FIG. 6, RED THREAD**).

CLASP: *String 2A, the top loop of one half of the clasp, and 2A; pass down through the last 2A exited on the rectangle component. Repeat the thread path to reinforce. Weave through beads to exit up through the side 2A of the unit below the last connection point (**FIG. 7, BLUE THREAD**). Repeat from *, connecting to the corresponding clasp loops (**FIG. 7, RED THREAD**). Secure the thread and trim.

Repeat Step 5 to connect the other side component to the right side of the center component. Repeat Step 6 to connect the right side of the other side component to the other rectangle component and other half of the clasp, making sure the clasp will close properly when worn.

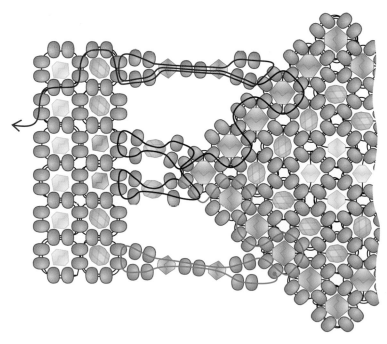

FIG. 6: Connecting the left side component to the rectangle component

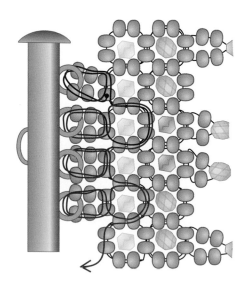

FIG. 7: Connecting the clasp

Rhythm of the Sea

Sára Zsadon

techniques

Cubic right-angle weave

Flat peyote stitch

Picot

Stringing

materials

1 g metallic blue size 15° seed beads (A)

13 g metallic blue size 11° seed beads (B)

5 g metallic bronze size 11° seed beads (C)

1 g metallic bronze size 8° seed beads (D)

20 metallic bronze 6mm pressed-glass rounds (E)

2 coils (about 14" [35.5 cm]) of gold 1¾–2¼"
    (4.5–5.5 cm) diameter bracelet memory wire

4 gold-plated 3mm oval screw-on wire end caps

Smoke 6 lb braided beading thread

tools

Scissors

Size 10 or 12 beading needles

Memory-wire cutters

1mm flat-head screwdriver

Pen or chopstick (optional)

finished size

6½" (16.5 cm) (adjustable)

1 Rope

Stitch a cubic-right-angle-weave rope:

CUBE 1, BOTTOM: Use 5' (1.5 m) of thread to string 4B, leaving a 12" (30.5 cm) tail; pass through the beads again to form a tight circle and tie a surgeon's knot to secure. Pass through the first B strung (**FIG. 1, BLACK THREAD**).

CUBE 1, FACE 1: String 3B; pass through the last B exited and the first B just added (**FIG. 1, ORANGE THREAD**).

CUBE 1, FACE 2: String 2B; pass back through the next bottom B, up through the nearest side B of Face 1, through the 2B just added, and the next bottom B (**FIG. 1, PURPLE THREAD**).

CUBE 1, FACE 3: String 2B; pass down through the nearest side B of Face 2, through the last bottom B exited, and up through the first B just added (**FIG. 1, GREEN THREAD**).

CUBE 1, FACE 4: String 1B; pass down through the nearest side B of Face 1, back through the next bottom B, up through the nearest side B of Face 3, and through the B just added (**FIG. 1, BLUE THREAD**).

CUBE 1, TOP: Pass through the 4 top B of the cube faces; pull the thread tight to complete the first cube (**FIG. 1, RED THREAD**).

CUBES 2–256: Repeat Cube 1, Faces 1–4 and the top, 255 times, using the top of the previous cube as the bottom of the new cube to form a cubic-right-angle-weave rope (**FIG. 2**). Don't trim the threads.

2 First End Loop

Form a loop on the end of the rope and embellish with peyote stitch:

JOIN: Bend the beginning of the rope so the bottom of Cube 1 touches a face of Cube 10. Use the tail thread, B, and cubic right-angle weave to connect the 2 cubes. Exit from a B along the inside edge of the loop just formed, toward Cube 10 (**FIG. 3**).

INSIDE, FRONT: String 1A and pass through the next inside-edge B; repeat nine times for a total of 10A. *NOTE: Choose the thinnest A beads for the inside of the loop. If the loop is too tight and there's not enough space for an A, you can broaden the loop with the help of a pen or a chopstick.* Weave through beads to exit from the outside-edge B of the joining unit, toward the outside of the loop (**FIG. 4, BLUE THREAD**).

OUTSIDE, FRONT: Work 3 peyote stitches with 2B in each stitch. Work 4 peyote stitches with 3C in each stitch, forming picots. Work 1 peyote stitch with 1B. String 1D and pass through the next B; weave through the beads on the side of the rope to reinforce this stitch again. *NOTE: Choose thinner beads when adding more than one at a time.* Weave through beads to exit from the mirror B on the outside edge of the back of the loop, toward the top of the loop (**FIG. 4, RED THREAD**). Flip the work over.

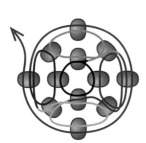

FIG. 1: Stitching the first cube

FIG. 2: Forming a cubic-right-angle-weave rope

FIG. 3: Joining the rope end to the rope side to form an end loop (only one face of the joining cube shown for clarity)

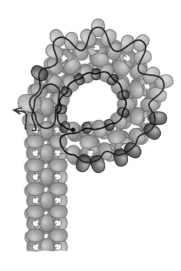

FIG. 4: Embellishing the edges of the front of the end loop

OUTSIDE, BACK: Work 1 stitch with 1D and reinforce as before, adding 1A between the 2B along the inside of the loop (**FIG. 5, GREEN THREAD**). Work 1 stitch with 1B and 7 stitches with 2B in each stitch. Weave through beads to exit from the nearest B on the inside-back edge of the loop, away from Cube 10 (**FIG. 5, BLUE THREAD**).

INSIDE, BACK: Work 8 stitches with 1A in each stitch, pass through the 1A added when reinforcing the D, then work 1 stitch with 1A. Weave through beads to exit away from the loop from a B below the D on the front of the rope (**FIG. 5, RED THREAD**).

③ Front Waves

Use peyote stitch to shape and embellish the front of the rope:

FRONT WAVE 1: Work peyote stitches along the front edge of the rope in the following stitch order: 1B six times, 1A six times, and 1B six times. *NOTE: This establishes the inner curve of the first wave on the front of the work.* Choose thin A beads so that the waves will be nicely arched.

Pass through the last D added on the front of the rope in the previous step and the next B along the edge so the rope forms a teardrop shape (**FIG. 6, GREEN THREAD**). Reinforce the D by passing through 2B on the face of the rope, adding 1B on the other side, and weaving through beads to exit from the B above the nearest D (**FIG. 6, BLUE THREAD**). *NOTE: Use this reinforcement method with all D, continuing to add 1B opposite the D as you stitch.*

FRONT WAVE 2: Work peyote stitches along the front edge of the rope in the following stitch order: 1B, 3C four times, 1B, and 1D. *NOTE: This establishes the outer curve of the second wave on the front of the work.* Reinforce the D, adding 1B on the other side as before (**FIG. 6, RED THREAD**).

FRONT WAVES 3–17: Repeat Waves 1 and 2 seven times, then repeat Wave 1.

FRONT WAVE 18: Repeat Wave 2, using 1B instead of 1D and omitting the reinforcement (**FIG. 7, GREEN THREAD**).

END: Work 4 peyote stitches with 1B in each stitch along the front edge on the end of the rope (**FIG. 7, BLUE THREAD**).

④ Second End Loop

Repeat the join in Step 2 to connect the final cube of the rope to the tenth-to-last cube (Cube 247), making sure the loop mirrors the first end loop (**FIG. 7, RED THREAD**). Repeat the inside and outside embellishments of Step 2 to complete the loop.

⑤ Opposite Waves, Front

Weave through beads to exit from the D added to the second end loop, away from the C embellishments. Pass through the next B along the inner edge of the rope. Repeat Step 3 along the unfinished front edge of the rope, forming waves that alternate with those already formed.

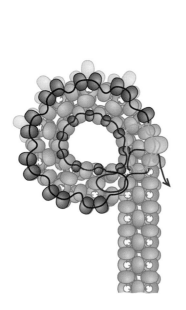

FIG. 5: Embellishing the edges of the back of the end loop

FIG. 6: Forming Waves 1 and 2 of the front of the bracelet

FIG. 7: Adding the end edge and closing the second loop (only one face of the joining cube shown for clarity)

6 Back Waves

Embellish the back edges of the waves to further structure the bracelet:

BACK WAVE 1: Weave through beads to exit from the first B along the outer edge on the back of the bracelet, under and away from the end loop. Work 10 peyote stitches with 1B in each stitch (**FIG. 8, ORANGE THREAD**). Work 1 stitch with 1D; reinforce the D, adding 1B to the other side as before (**FIG. 8, GREEN THREAD**).

BACK WAVE 2: Work 6 peyote stitches with 1B in each stitch, 1 peyote stitch with 1A, and then pass through the next 4B without adding any beads. Work 1 peyote stitch with 1A and 6 peyote stitches with 1B in each stitch. Reinforce the last D added, adding 1B to the other side as before (**FIG. 8, BLUE THREAD**).

BACK WAVE 3: Work 6 peyote stitches with 1B in each stitch. Work 1 peyote stitch with 1D; reinforce the D, adding 1B to the other side as before (**FIG. 8, RED THREAD**).

BACK WAVES 4–17: Repeat Back Waves 2 and 3 seven times.

BACK WAVE 18: Repeat Back Wave 2.

OPPOSITE BACK WAVES: Rotate the bracelet and repeat Back Waves 1–18 on the other edge of the bracelet's back, incorporating the B that were added to the first edge as necessary. Secure the thread and trim.

7 Assembly

Place memory wire inside the beadwork to give it structure:

CUT: Cut 2 coils of memory wire. Screw 1 end cap on one end of each wire.

STRING: Place 1E inside the first end loop of the bracelet. Push 1 wire through the center of the third unit on the end loop (right below the first picot made from C, counted up from the joining unit). Push the wire through the E just placed at the center of the loop, and continue through to the other side of this and the next wave. *NOTE: The wire will sit behind the D. If the wire doesn't slip easily through the cubes, you may need to pull the beads away from the wire with the help of a beading needle.*

Push the second wire through the center of the first wave's fifth unit (counted down from the joining unit). Push it through the rope, string 1B, 1E, and 1B, and push it forward through the walls of the next 2 waves. *NOTE: To make it easier to add the beads between waves, first push the wire through the rope; string the B/E/B, hold the last B and the end of the wire with the nail of your index finger, and gently push back the wire with your other hand, taking care so the beads don't slip down. Place the wire with the beads into the wave and push it through the rope. If needed, use flat-nose pliers to help push/pull the wire.*

Continue stringing 1B, 1E, and 1B into the next wave on both the top and bottom of the bracelet, alternating the wires by each step (**FIG. 9**). String 1E into the second end loop; then screw 1 end cap on the open end of each wire.

Fig. 8: Stitching Back Waves 1–3

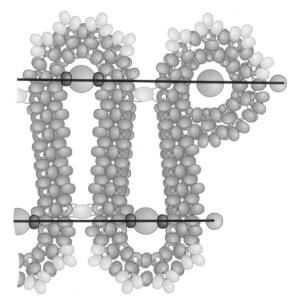

Fig. 9: Stringing the bracelet

Artist's Tips

- Besides screw-on end caps, there are different solutions to finish the memory-wire ends. You can use glue-on end caps or simply curl the wire into a tight simple loop with round-nose pliers.

- Even good-quality seed beads tend to be uneven in size, but it comes in handy when peyote-stitching the waves. For a nice result, take care to use thinner-than-average size 15°s for the inner arches of the waves and use wider size 11°s for the outside of the waves.

- You can omit the memory wire and finish the bracelet with thread. Just use thread to string the body of the bracelet and attach magnetic clasps to the ends. This makes a looser bracelet, but is easier than stringing with the memory wire.

- When working the rope, you can make counting the units easier by using safety pins or stitch markers; stitch one pin into the center of every twentieth cube.

- If you find the arch of the wave too narrow for stringing the beads between waves, pull it wider with your fingers.

- You can use the tip of a screwdriver to guide the wire between the B beads.

13

Paradox

Nichole Starman

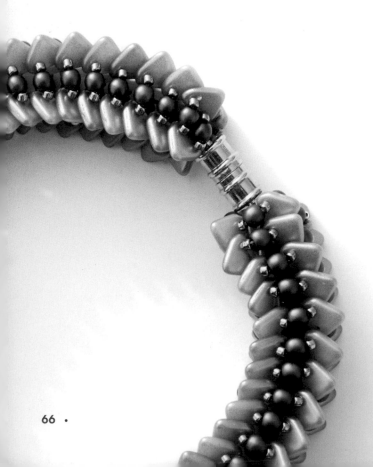

technique

Tubular netting variation

materials

2 g nickel size 15° Japanese seed beads (A)

196 halo ethereal shadows 6mm flat 2-hole front-drilled triangles (B)

200 steel blue 3mm glass pearl rounds (C)

1 silver 5×18mm magnetic cylinder clasp

Gray nylon beading thread

tools

Scissors

Size 12 beading needle

finished size

9" (23 cm)

① Rope

Use a variation of tubular netting to form a dimensional rope:

ROUND 1: Lay 4B on your work surface with the holes nearest you and the top point of each B facing away. Use 8' (2.4 m) of thread to string the right hole of 1B, 1A, 1C, and 1A; repeat three times, leaving a 6" (15 cm) tail. Use the working and tail threads to tie a knot, forming a tight circle. Repeat the thread path of this round. Pass through the first (inside) hole of the first B strung and the next 1A/1C/1A/1B (inside hole). Step up through the second (outside) hole of the current B (**FIG. 1**). *NOTE: You'll now begin working in the opposite direction. All illustrations show a bird's-eye view of the rope; hold the work so you're looking down toward the center opening as you bead.*

ROUND 2: *NOTE: In this round, string each new B through the left hole.* Lay 4B on your work surface with the holes nearest you and the top point of each B facing away. String 1B, 1A, 1C, 1A, and 1B; pass through the next B (outside hole) of the previous round. String 1A, 1C, and 1A; pass through the next B (outside hole) of the previous round (**FIG. 2, BLUE THREAD**). Repeat from the beginning of this round. Repeat the thread path of this round. Pass through the first 1B (inside hole)/1A/1C/1A/1B (inside then outside holes) added. *NOTE: You'll now begin working in the opposite direction* (**FIG. 2, RED THREAD**).

ROUND 3: *NOTE: In this round, string each new B through the right hole.* Lay 4B on your work surface with the holes nearest you and the top point of each B facing away. String 1B, 1A, 1C, 1A, and 1B; pass through the next B (outside hole) of the previous round. String 1A, 1C, and 1A; pass through the next B (outside hole) of the previous round. Repeat from the beginning of this round. Repeat the thread path of this round. Pass through the first 1B (inside hole)/1A/1C/1A/1B (inside then outside holes) added. *NOTE: You'll now begin working in the opposite direction* (**FIG. 3**).

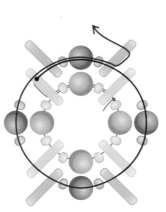
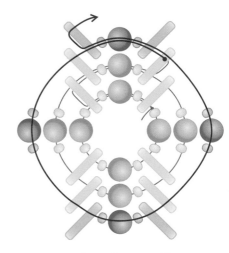

FIG. 1: Stitching Round 1 **FIG. 2:** Working Round 2 **FIG. 3:** Adding Round 3

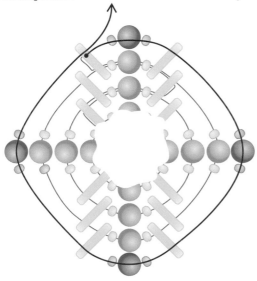
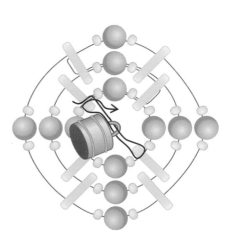

FIG. 4: Forming Round 50 **FIG. 5:** Attaching the clasp

ROUNDS 4–49: Repeat Rounds 2 and 3 twenty-three times.

ROUND 50: String 1A, 1C, and 1A and pass through the next B (outside hole) of the previous round; repeat three times (**FIG. 4**). Repeat the thread path of this round to reinforce. Secure the threads and trim.

2 Clasp

Add a needle to the center of 2' (0.6 m) of new thread and bring the ends together to form a 12" (30.5 cm) doubled thread. Secure the thread so it exits from the inside hole of 1B in Round 48, leaving a 4" (10 cm) tail. String one half of the clasp; pass through the diagonal B (inside hole) of Round 48, back through the clasp, and through the last B (inside hole) exited (**FIG. 5**). Repeat the thread path to reinforce. Secure the threads and trim. Repeat this step on the other end of the bracelet, working off of the B of Round 2 and using the other half of the clasp.

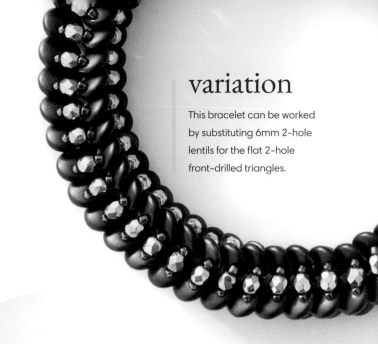

variation

This bracelet can be worked by substituting 6mm 2-hole lentils for the flat 2-hole front-drilled triangles.

Artist's Tips

- When attaching the clasp, string 4A, one half of the clasp, and 4A to add flexibility to the attachment.

- One-G thread is ideal for both the lentil and the triangle versions because it's strong, forms a tight stitch, and has many color shades to choose from. FireLine works best for the crescent version because it creates a more flexible stitch. Crescent beads are longer and thinner than triangles or lentils, requiring more wiggle room between beads.

variation

This bracelet can be worked by substituting 3x10mm 2-hole crescent beads for the flat 2-hole front-drilled triangles. In each round, lay 4 crescent beads horizontally on your work surface with each bead's inside curve facing downward; alternate between stringing the right and left holes of the crescents with each round as done in the main version. For a bracelet that measures 9¼" (23.5 cm), work 44 rounds.

That's a Wrap!

Jann Christiansen

techniques

Right-angle weave

Netting

materials

7 g metallic bright bronze size 11° seed beads (A)

6 g metallic bronze 2.8mm Japanese drops (B)*

112 rainbow 4×3mm crystal rondelles (C)

2 antiqued brass 4mm wireguards

1 antiqued bronze 8×16mm ball-and-socket clasp

2 antiqued brass 5mm jump rings

Smoke 8 lb FireLine braided beading thread

** You can substitute 3mm magatama drops for the 2.8mm Japanese drops.
Experiment with other types of rondelles for a variety of looks.*

tools

Scissors

Size 11 beading needle

2 pairs of chain- or flat-nose pliers

finished size

21¼" (54 cm)

① Base

Use right-angle weave to stitch the base of the bracelet:

UNIT 1: Use 6' (1.8 m) of thread to string 8A, leaving a 6" (15 cm) tail. Pass through the beads again to form a tight circle; use the working and tail threads to tie a knot. Pass through the first 6A strung (**FIG. 1, GREEN THREAD**).

UNIT 2: String 6A and pass through the last 2A exited in the previous unit and the first 4A of this unit (**FIG. 1, BLUE THREAD**).

UNITS 3–112: Repeat Unit 2 one hundred ten times for a total of 112 units (**FIG. 1, RED THREAD**).

② Center Embellishment

String 1C and pass up through the mirror 2A of the previous unit in the base (**FIG. 2, TURQUOISE THREAD**); repeat 111 times. Pass through the nearest 2A at the top edge of the base (**FIG. 2, RED THREAD**).

③ Edges

String 1B and pass through the nearest 2A along the same edge of the base (**FIG. 3, GREEN THREAD**); repeat 110 times. Weave through beads to exit from the nearest 2A at the opposite edge of the base (**FIG. 3, BLUE THREAD**). Repeat from the beginning of this step (**FIG. 3, RED THREAD**). Secure the threads and trim.

④ Clasp

Start 14" (35.5 cm) of new thread that exits up through the outside 2A at one end of the base, leaving a 4" (10 cm) tail. String 1A, 1 wireguard, and 1A; pass through the last 2A exited on the base (**FIG. 4**). Repeat the thread path of this step to reinforce. Secure the threads and trim. Use 1 jump ring to attach one half of the clasp to the previous wireguard.

Repeat this entire step at the other end of the base, using the second half of the clasp.

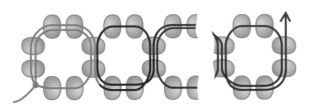

FIG. 1: Forming the base

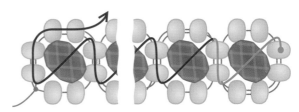

FIG. 2: Embellishing the center

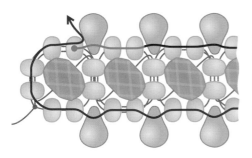

FIG. 3: Stitching the edges

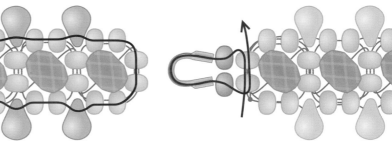

FIG. 4: Attaching the clasp

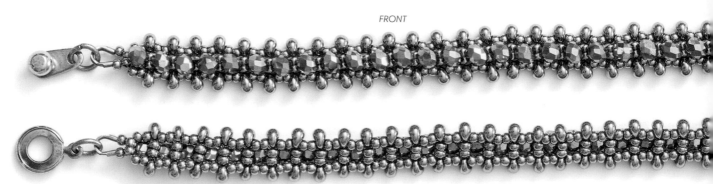

FRONT

BACK

MAIN COLORWAY

Artist's Tips

- Loosen your tension if the base starts to twist while you're stitching the center embellishment.

- Reinforce the thread path of Step 2 to make sure the crystal rondelles are secured to the base.

alternate colorway materials

7 g metallic nickel size 11° seed beads (A)

222 nickel 3mm magatama drops (B)

112 silver 4×3mm crystal rondelles (C)

2 antiqued silver 4mm wireguards

1 silver 8×16mm ball-and-socket clasp

2 antiqued silver 5mm jump rings

Smoke 8 lb FireLine braided beading thread

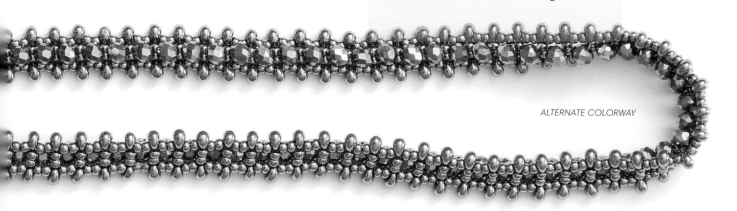

ALTERNATE COLORWAY

Formal Affair

Leslee Frumin

techniques

Right-angle weave variation

Netting

materials

3 g bronze size 15° Japanese seed beads (A)

8 bronze size 11° Japanese seed beads (B)

56 white opal AB 2×3mm crystal bicones (C)

48 bright gold 4mm crystal pearl rounds (D)

Smoke 6 lb braided beading thread

tools

Scissors

Size 12 beading needles

finished size

6⅜" (16.5 cm)

① Strips

Use a right-angle weave variation with pearls and seed beads to stitch 2 identical strips:

STRIP 1, UNIT 1: Use 7' (2.1 m) of thread to string 7A and 1D, leaving a 4' (1.2 m) tail; pass through all the beads again (**FIG. 1, BLUE THREAD**). String 7A and pass through the last D added; repeat the thread path to reinforce and exit from the first 4A just added (**FIG. 1, RED THREAD**).

STRIP 1, UNIT 2: String 3A, 1D, and 3A, then pass through the last A exited from the previous stitch; repeat the thread path to reinforce and exit from the D just added (**FIG. 2, BLUE THREAD**). String 7A and pass through the last D exited; repeat the thread path to reinforce and exit from the first 4A just added (**FIG. 2, RED THREAD**).

STRIP 1, UNITS 3–19: Repeat Strip 1, Unit 2, seventeen times or to the desired length minus ½" (1.3 cm) for the clasp. Secure the working thread, but don't trim the tail thread; set aside.

Strip 2: Repeat Strip 1 for a second strip.

② Connect

Embellish and weave the pearl strips together to form the bracelet base:

EDGE EMBELLISHMENT: Add a needle to the tail thread of 1 strip. Weave through beads to exit from the seventh A of Unit 1, toward the work. *String 1A; pass back through the next A (**FIG. 3, GREEN THREAD**). String 1A, 1C, and 1A; pass through the A before the open space over the next D (**FIG. 3, BLUE THREAD**). Repeat from * seventeen times for a total of 18A. String 1A and pass down through the 7A at the end of the strip (**FIG. 3, RED THREAD**). Don't trim the thread; set aside. Repeat from the beginning of this step for the second strip.

CONNECT: Arrange the strips horizontally so that the embellished side of the top strip touches the non-embellished side of the bottom one. Use the bottom thread to pass through the first edge embellishment A of the top strip and the next A of the bottom strip (**FIG. 4, GREEN THREAD**). *Pass through the next 1A/1C/1A of the top strip and into the A before the open space over the next D of the bottom strip (**FIG. 4, BLUE THREAD**). Pass through the next edge embellishment A of the top strip and the next A of the bottom strip. Repeat from * seventeen times or to the end of the base to connect the top and bottom strips (**FIG. 4, RED THREAD**), then repeat the thread path to reinforce. *NOTE: Because the edge embellishments may slightly shorten the base, it's best to retest the base now for fit. If necessary, add units to each strip and then connect them in the same manner.*

FIG. 1: Forming Strip 1, Unit 1

FIG. 2: Adding Strip 1, Unit 2

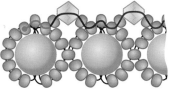

FIG. 3: Stitching the first edge embellishment

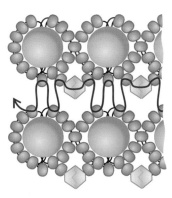
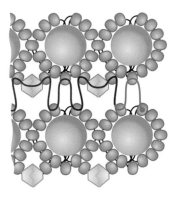

FIG. 4: Connecting the top and bottom strips

TOP EDGE: Repeat the edge embellishment to finish the top edge of the top strip. Secure the thread and trim. Set the work aside.

3 Clasp Button

Use netting to form a button for the clasp:

RING: Use 3' (0.9 m) of thread to string {1D and 1B} eight times, leaving a 6" (15 cm) tail. Pass through all the beads again to form a tight circle; tie a square knot to secure, and pass through the first 1D/1B added to hide the knot within the beadwork (**FIG. 5, BLUE THREAD**).

NETS: String 5A and pass through the next B of the ring; repeat twice, then pass through the nearest 1D/1B (**FIG. 5, RED THREAD**). Press the nets just formed toward the inside of the ring, then manipulate the ring into an oblong shape.

CENTER: String 2A; pass back through the middle A of the last net formed (**FIG. 6, PURPLE THREAD**). String 2A; pass through the next B of the ring to form an X (**FIG. 6, GREEN THREAD**). String 2A, pass back through the middle A of the next net, then string 2A and pass through the next B of the ring to form the second X (**FIG. 6, BLUE THREAD**); repeat to form the third X. Pass through the nearest 1D/1B/3A (**FIG. 6, RED THREAD**).

TOP EMBELLISHMENT: String 1A, 1C, and 1A; pass through the center A of the next X formed in the center; repeat (**FIG. 7, BLUE THREAD**). Weave through beads to exit back through the last 1A/1C/1A added. String 1A; pass back through the first 1A/1C/1A, then weave through the following 3A/1B/1D/1B (**FIG. 7, RED THREAD**). Turn the button over.

BACK: String 1A, 1D, and 1A and pass through the mirror B on the other side of the ring, back through the 1A/1D/1A just added, and through the first B exited and the next 1D/1B of the ring (**FIG. 8, BLUE THREAD**); repeat to add a second set of 1A/1D/1A (**FIG. 8, RED THREAD**). Secure the thread and trim. *NOTE: Because the beadwork is so tight, it may be helpful to pass through the beads at an angle.*

MAIN COLORWAY

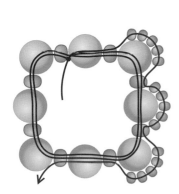

FIG. 5: Forming the ring and nets of the clasp button

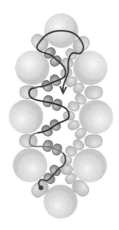

FIG. 6: Stitching the center of the clasp button

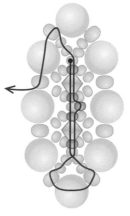

FIG. 7: Embellishing the clasp button

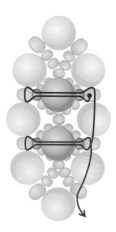

FIG. 8: Adding beads to the back of the button

CONNECT: Start 12" (30.5 cm) of new thread that exits an end D of the base's Strip 1, toward the center of the beadwork. String 5A; pass through a 1A/1D/1A combination on the back of the button. String 1A; pass back through the last 1A/1D/1A exited (**FIG. 9, GREEN THREAD**). String 5A; pass through the last D exited in Strip 1 (**FIG. 9, BLUE THREAD**). String 2A and pass through the end D of the base's Strip 2. String 5A; pass through the next 1A/1D/1A combination on the back of the button. String 1A; pass back through the last 1A/1D/1A exited. String 5A; pass through the last D exited in Strip 2 (**FIG. 9, RED THREAD**). Repeat the entire thread path twice to reinforce. Secure the thread and trim.

④ Clasp Loop

Start 12" (30.5 cm) of new thread that exits from the other end D of the base's Strip 2, toward the edge of the beadwork. String 31A or enough to accommodate the button; pass through the end D of Strip 1, toward the center of the base. String 2A; pass through the end D of Strip 2 (**FIG. 10**). Repeat the thread path three times to reinforce. Secure the thread and trim.

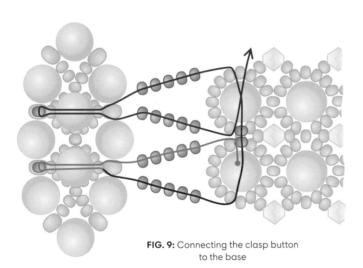

FIG. 9: Connecting the clasp button to the base

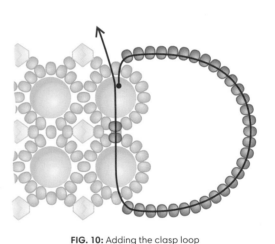

FIG. 10: Adding the clasp loop

ALTERNATE COLORWAY

ALTERNATE COLORWAY

Artist's Tip

- Although Japanese seed beads
  are consistent in size, there is
  variation in size between colors
  and manufacturers, and this can
  affect the ultimate size of your
  piece. Be sure to test the bracelet's
  fit before adding the button and
  loop closure.

variation

Form a wider cuff by adding
a third row of pearls to the base
and stitching a wider clasp.

Lilac Lace

Yasmin Sarfati

techniques

Right-angle weave

Netting

materials

5 g gold-luster pale wisteria size 11° seed beads (A)

91 mauve 4mm crystal pearl rounds (B)

182 silver night 4mm crystal bicones (C)

6 silver 20-gauge 6.5mm jump rings

3 antiqued silver 6×9mm magnetic clasps

Purple size D nylon beading thread

tools

Scissors

Size 11 or 12 beading needles

finished size

7¾" (19.5 cm)

1 Band

Use right-angle weave to stitch the bracelet band:

ROW 1, BASE: Use 6' (1.8 m) of thread and B to right-angle-weave a row 30 units long or to the desired length minus ½" (1.3 cm) for the clasp.

ROW 1, EMBELLISHMENT, FIRST PASS:
Exiting down through the end B of the Row 1 base, *string 7A; pass up through the nearest side B of the previous unit to form a loop. String 7A; pass down through the side B of the following unit to form another loop. Repeat from * down the base (**FIG. 1**).

ROW 1, EMBELLISHMENT, SECOND PASS:
Exiting down through the end B of the base, string 5A; pass up through the last 2A of the nearest loop on this side of the base, the nearest side B of the base, and the first 2A of the nearest loop on the other side of the base (**FIG. 2, GREEN THREAD**). **String 3A; pass down through the last 2A of the nearest loop on this side of the base, the nearest side B of the base, and the last 2A of the nearest loop on the other side of the base.

Repeat from ** across the base (**FIG. 2, BLUE THREAD**). For the final stitch, string 5A and pass down through the end B of the base (**FIG. 2, RED THREAD**). Set aside.

ROW 2, BASE: Repeat Row 1, base, using C.

ROW 2, EMBELLISHMENT, FIRST PASS:
Exiting down through the final C of the Row 2 base, *string 7A; pass up through the next side C of the Row 2 base to form a loop. String 3A; pass through the middle A of the second-from-the-right loop of 7A at the bottom of Row 1. String 3A; pass down through the next side C of the Row 2 base (**FIG. 3, BLUE THREAD**). Repeat from * to the end of the base, connecting to every other 7A bottom loop of Row 1 (**FIG. 3, RED THREAD**).

ROW 2, EMBELLISHMENT, SECOND PASS:
Exiting down through the end C of the Row 2 base, string 5A; pass up through the last 2A of the next bottom loop, the nearest side C, and the first 2A of the nearest top loop (**FIG. 4, GREEN THREAD**). **String 1A; pass through the middle A of the next 7A loop at the bottom of Row 1, toward the work. String 1A; pass down through the last 2A of the next loop on

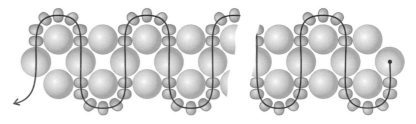

FIG. 1: Adding the first pass of embellishment for Row 1

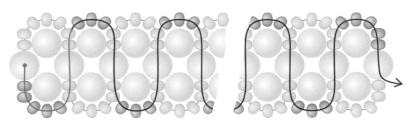

FIG. 2: Stitching the second pass of embellishment for Row 1

the top of the Row 2 base, the next side C, and the first 2A of the nearest loop on the bottom of the Row 2 base. String 3A; pass up through the last 2A of the nearest loop on the bottom of the Row 2 base, the next C, and the first 2A of the nearest loop on the top of the Row 2 base. Repeat from ** across the base of Row 2 (**FIG. 4, BLUE THREAD**). For the final stitch, string 1A; pass through the middle A of the final 7A loop at the bottom of Row 1. String 3A; pass down through the end C of the Row 2 base (**FIG. 4, RED THREAD**). Secure the thread and trim.

ROW 3: Repeat the Row 2 base and embellishments, this time connecting to the other side of Row 1.

② Clasp

Start 2' (0.6 m) of new thread that exits down through an end C of Row 3. String 6A; pass through the last C exited, then repeat the thread path twice to reinforce. Weave through beads to exit down through the end B of Row 1. String 6A; pass through the last B exited, then repeat the thread path twice to reinforce. Weave through beads to exit through the end C of Row 2. String 6A; pass through the last C exited, then repeat the thread path twice to reinforce. Secure the thread and trim. Use 1 jump ring to connect one half of 1 clasp to each loop (**FIG. 5**). Repeat this entire step on the other end of the bracelet.

Artist's Tips

- For a more delicate look, use 3mm beads in place of the 4mm beads. You will need to adjust the number of beads in the embellishments accordingly.

- Mix and match different colors and types of 4mm beads to get a different bracelet every time.

- For a thin bracelet, only work Row 1. For a wider bracelet, continue adding rows.

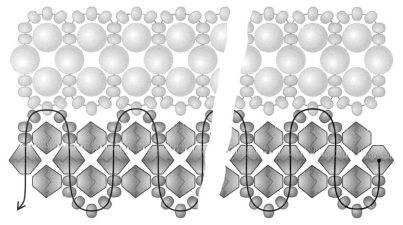

FIG. 3: Adding the first embellishment pass of Row 2

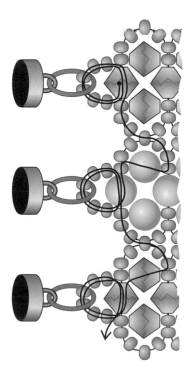

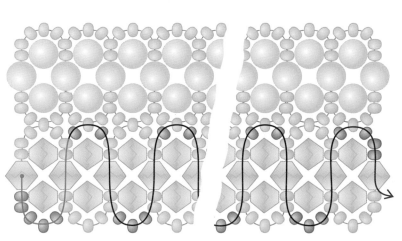

FIG. 4: Forming the second embellishment pass of Row 2

FIG. 5: Adding the clasp loops

Lily Pad

Sandie Bachand

techniques

Ladder stitch

Brick stitch variation

Netting

Right-angle weave variation

Fringe

materials

2 g matte turquoise iris size 15° seed beads (A)

0.5 g opaque black size 15° seed beads (B)

13 peridot 6mm crystal roses monteés (C)

27 matte brown iris 6mm Czech flat 2-hole squares (D)

50 metallic light green suede 6mm 2-hole triangle beads (E)

164 gray 2mm (small) glass pearls (F)

76 gray 3mm (large) glass pearls (G)

1 antiqued brass 5×10mm barrel clasp

Smoke 6 lb braided beading thread

tools

Scissors

Size 12 beading needle

finished size

7⅜" (19 cm)

❶ Base

Use ladder stitch and a brick stitch variation to form the base:

CENTER: Use 6' (1.8 m) of thread to string 2D, leaving a 6" (15 cm) tail; pass through the beads again and manipulate them so they sit side by side. Pass through the second (right) hole of the second D (**FIG. 1, BLUE THREAD**). *String 1D; pass through the right hole of the last D exited, through the same (left) hole of the D just added, and through the right hole of the same D (**FIG. 1, RED THREAD**). Repeat from * twenty-four times for a total of 27D, but do not pass through the right hole of the final D. Pass through the right hole of the second-to-last D.

EDGES: String 1E; pass back through the right hole of the last D exited. String 1E; pass through the right hole of the last D exited and through the left hole of the same D (**FIG. 2, BLUE THREAD**). Pass through the left hole of the nearest E and back through the left hole of the last D exited. Pass through the left hole of the first E, through the left hole of the D, and through the right hole of the next D in

the base (**FIG. 2, RED THREAD**). Repeat from the beginning of Edges twenty-four times for a total of 50E, but do not pass through the right hole of the final D.

❷ Top Embellishment

Use fringe, netting, and a right-angle weave variation to embellish the top of the base:

PASS 1: String 1C; pass down through the right hole of the last D exited. Pass through the second hole of the last C added, down through the left hole of the last D exited, and up through the right hole of the D (**FIG. 3**, blue thread). Weave through the next D of the base (without adding beads) to pass down through the left hole of the following D (**FIG. 3, RED THREAD**). Repeat from the beginning of Pass 1 twelve times for a total of 13C, but do not weave through the final D at the end of the base. Pass through the nearest hole of the last C added.

PASS 2, UNIT 1: String 1F, 1G, and 1F; pass through the bottom right hole of the last C exited. String 1F, 1G, and 1F; pass through the bottom left hole of the

C. String 1F, 1G, and 1F; pass through the top left hole of the C. String 1F, 1G, and 1F; pass through the top right hole of the C (**FIG. 4, BLUE THREAD**). Pass through all the beads of this unit in a counterclockwise direction and exit down through the leftmost G of this unit (**FIG. 4, RED THREAD**).

PASS 2, UNIT 2: String 3G; pass through the last G exited in the previous unit and the first G just added (**FIG. 5, FRONT, GREEN THREAD**). String 3A, 1B, and 3A; pass through the last G exited and the left hole of the nearest E to exit from the back of the base. String 4A; pass through the right hole of the E, the last G exited, and the following 2G (**FIG. 5, FRONT AND BACK, BLUE THREADS**). String 3A, 1B, and 3A; pass through the last G exited and the right hole of the nearest E to exit from the back of the base. String 4A; pass through the left hole of the E, the last G exited, and the following 3G (**FIG. 5, FRONT AND BACK, RED THREADS**).

PASS 2, UNIT 3: String 1F; pass through the top right hole of the nearest C. String 1F, 1G, and 1F; pass through the bottom

FIG. 1: Beginning the center of the base

FIG. 2: Adding the edges of the base

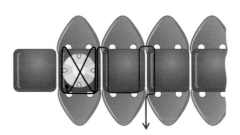

FIG. 3: Working Pass 1 of the top embellishment

FIG. 4: Forming Pass 2, Unit 1 of the top embellishment

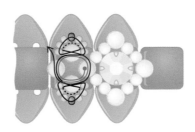

FIG. 5: FRONT. Stitching Pass 2, Unit 2, of the top embellishment

FIG. 5: BACK. Working on the back of the triangles

right hole of the C (**FIG. 6, PURPLE THREAD**). String 1F, 1G, and 1F; pass through the bottom left hole of the C (Fig. 6, green thread). String 1F, 1G, and 1F; pass through the top left hole of the nearest C. String 1F; pass through the last G exited in the previous unit and the first F of this unit (**FIG. 6, BLUE THREAD**). Pass through all the beads of this unit in a counterclockwise direction and exit down through the leftmost G of this unit (**FIG. 6, RED THREAD**).

PASS 2, UNITS 3–25: Repeat Pass 2, Units 2 and 3 eleven times. Pass through the nearest 2F of the final unit and the left hole of the nearest E to exit from the back of the base.

③ Back Embellishment

Turn the beadwork facedown. String 4A and 1F; pass through the next 4A along the back of the base. String 1F, 4A, and 1F, then pass through the next 4A along the back of the base; repeat ten times. String 1F and 4A; pass through the right hole of the final E. Weave through beads to exit from the right hole of the nearest E on the other

edge of the bracelet (**FIG. 7, BLUE THREAD**). Turn the bracelet 180 degrees and repeat this entire step (**FIG. 7, RED THREAD**). Weave through beads to exit from the nearest end G of the top embellishment.

④ Clasp

Turn the beadwork faceup. String 2F; pass through the left hole of the end D. String 2F; pass through the last G exited, the first 2F of this step, and the left hole of the D (**FIG. 8, BLUE THREAD**). String 1A, 1F, one half of the clasp, 1F, and 1A; pass through the left hole of the D (**FIG. 8, RED THREAD**). Repeat the entire thread path to reinforce. Secure the working thread and trim. Add a needle to the tail thread and weave through beads to exit from the end G, then repeat this entire step using the other half of the clasp. Secure the thread and trim.

MAIN COLORWAY

Artist's Tip

- Use loose enough tension when stitching the base row of square beads to allow adequate space for the pearl embellishments around the crystal roses monteés.

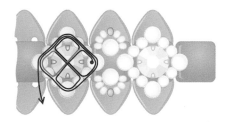

FIG. 6: Working Pass 2, Unit 3 of the top embellishment

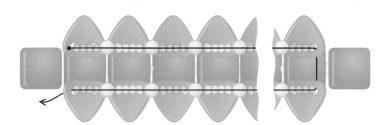

FIG. 7: Adding the back embellishment

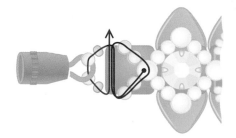

FIG. 8: Attaching one half of the clasp

Xs and Os

Maria Teresa Moran

techniques

Two-needle right-angle weave

Netting

materials

5 g bronze size 11° seed beads (A)

20 indicolite 3mm crystal bicones (B)

32 light amethyst Dorado 4mm crystal bicones (C)

36 powder rose 4mm crystal pearls (D)

9 Bordeaux 10mm crystal pearls (E)

10 light smoky topaz 6mm fire-polished rounds (F)

1 gold pewter 12×15mm fancy toggle clasp

Smoke 8 lb braided beading thread

tools

Scissors

Size 12 beading needles

finished size

7" (18 cm)

① Base

Use two-needle right-angle weave to form the bracelet base:

UNIT 1: Place one needle on each end of 6' (1.8 m) of thread. Use the right needle to string 1F, 1A, 1D, 1A, and 1E. Use the left needle to string 1A, 1D, and 1A, then pass back through the last E added to form the first unit (**FIG. 1, GREEN THREAD**). *NOTE: Because of the nature of two-needle right-angle weave, the needles will switch left and right positions with each stitch.*

UNIT 2: Use the right needle to string 1A, 1D, 1A, and 1F. Use the left needle to string 1A, 1D, and 1A, then pass back through the last F added to form the second unit (**FIG. 1, BLUE THREAD**).

UNIT 3: Use the right needle to string 1A, 1D, 1A, and 1E. Use the left needle to string 1A, 1D, and 1A, then pass back through the last E added to form the third unit (**FIG. 1, RED THREAD**).

UNITS 4–18: Repeat Units 2 and 3 seven times or to the desired length minus 1½" (3.8 cm) for the final unit and clasp. Repeat Unit 2 again for a total of 18 units. Weave through beads so a thread exits from each side of the final E placed.

② Crisscrosses

Add a crisscross layer of embellishment over the top of the base:

STITCH 1: Turn the base so the final E added points down. Use the right needle to string 3A, 1C, and 1A. Use the left needle to string 3A and 1C; pass through the final A added to the right needle (**FIG. 2, BLUE THREAD**).

STITCH 2: Use the right needle to string 1C and 3A, then pass through the next E on the base; repeat with the left needle, passing through the E in the opposite direction (**FIG. 2, RED THREAD**).

STITCHES 3–16: Repeat Stitches 1 and 2 seven times for a total of 8 crisscrosses. Weave through beads to exit from the F at the end of the base, with one thread exiting each side.

③ Clasp Ring

Use the right needle to string 3A, 1B, 3A, the clasp ring, and 3A; pass back through the B just added. String 3A; pass through the F at the end of the base and the nearest 1A/1D/1A (**FIG. 3, BLUE THREAD**). Use the left needle to retrace the thread path of the right needle, working in the opposite direction to exit from the opposite 1A/1D/1A (**FIG. 3, RED THREAD**).

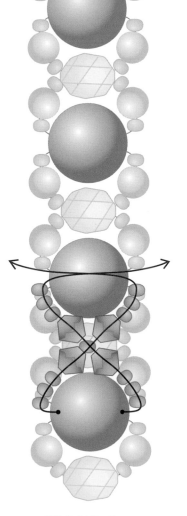

FIG. 1: Stitching Units 1–3 of the base

FIG. 2: Adding the crisscrosses to the base

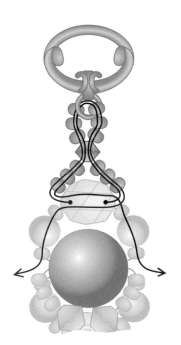

FIG. 3: Attaching the clasp ring

④ Edge Embellishment

Turn the bracelet so the clasp ring points down. *Use the right needle to string 1B, then pass through the next 1A/1D/2A/1D/1A along the right side of the base (**FIG. 4, BLUE THREAD**). Use the left needle to repeat from * on the left side of the base (**FIG. 4, RED THREAD**). Continue adding B on each side of the base in this manner, keeping the thread tension even, for a total of 8B on each side. For the final stitch, use the right needle to string 1B and pass through the next 1A/1D/1A/1F at the end of the base; repeat with the left needle (**FIG. 5**).

⑤ Clasp Bar

Repeat Step 3, this time adding the clasp bar. Secure the thread and trim.

Artist's Tip

- As you embellish the sides in Step 4, you may find it helpful to work a few stitches on one side and then a couple on the other side. This will help keep even tension so the finished bracelet lines up straight.

ALTERNATE COLORWAY

MAIN COLORWAY

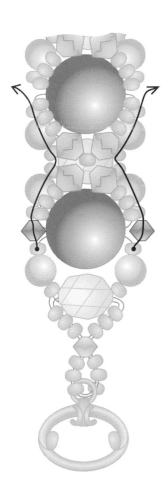

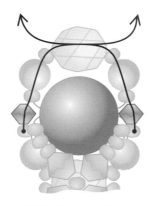

FIG. 4: Adding the edge embellishments

FIG. 5: Stitching the final edge embellishments and setting up to add the clasp bar

Forest Sprite

Barbara Falkowitz

techniques

Right-angle weave variation

Picot

materials

2 g red-lined rust size 15° seed beads (A)

2 g metallic teal size 15° seed beads (B)

5 g matte golden iris size 11° seed beads (C)

5 g aqua Picasso 5×2.5mm tapered 2-hole seed beads (D)

10 opaque rust 4mm pressed-glass rounds (E)

10 opaque green luster 6mm fire-polished rounds (F)

5 light Colorado topaz 3mm crystal rose montées (G)

20 padparadscha satin 4mm crystal bicones (H)

1 antiqued brass 12×10mm 2-strand filigree box clasp

Smoke 6 lb braided beading thread

tools

Scissors

Size 10 beading needle

finished size

7½" (19 cm)

① Small Components

Use a variation of right-angle weave to form the first component:

ROUND 1: Use 3' (0.9 m) of thread to string {1C and 1D} four times, leaving a 6" (15 cm) tail; pass through the beads again to form a circle. Tie a strong knot with the working and tail threads; pass through the nearest C (**FIG. 1, BLUE THREAD**).

CENTER: String 1G; pass through the 1C opposite the last C exited and the next 1D and 1C. Pass through the second channel in the G, through the 1C opposite the last C exited, and the nearest D. Step up through the outside hole of the D (**FIG. 1, RED THREAD**). *NOTE: You will now begin working clockwise.*

ROUND 2: String 1C, 1H, and 1C and pass through the outside hole of the next 1D of Round 1; repeat three times. Weave through beads to exit from the first 1H added in this round (**FIG. 2, BLUE THREAD**).

ROUND 3: String 1B, 1C, 3D, 1C, and 1B; pass through the last H exited to form a loop, then pass through the next 1C/1D/1C/1H. Repeat from the beginning of this round twice. String 1B, 1C, 3D, 1C, and 1B; pass through the last H exited to form a loop. Weave through beads to exit from the second 1C just added (**FIG. 2, RED THREAD**).

ROUND 4: String 1F; pass through the next 1C/3D/1C. String 1E; pass through the next 1C/3D/1C. Repeat from the beginning of this round. Pass through the first 1F added in this round (**FIG. 3, BLUE THREAD**).

ROUND 5: String 1B, 1C, 1D, 1C, 1D, 1C, and 1B and pass through the last 1F exited so the beads just added wrap around the outside of the 1F; repeat the thread path to reinforce. Weave through beads to exit the next F of Round 4. Repeat from the beginning of this round once. Weave through beads to exit from the first 1C added in this round (**FIG. 3, RED THREAD**). Don't trim the thread. Set the small component aside.

Repeat this entire step three times for a total of 4 small components.

② Large Component

Repeat Rounds 1–4 of the small component. Repeat Round 5, but instead of embellishing only the F of Round 4, also embellish the E; omit the first and third C when adding the beads that wrap around the E. Set the large component aside.

③ Connect

Stitch the components together:

LINK 1: Use the working thread of 1 small component to string 3A; pass through the outside hole of the nearest D (**FIG. 4, PURPLE THREAD**). String 1B, 1D, and 1B; pass up through the outside hole of the mirror D on a second small component (**FIG. 4, GREEN THREAD**). String 3A; pass through the inside hole of the D just exited and weave through beads to exit from the inside hole of the next D in the same round (**FIG. 4, BLUE THREAD**). String 3A; pass through the outside hole of the D just exited. String 1B; pass through the bottom hole of the D added at the beginning of this link. String 1B; pass through the outside hole of the mirror D on the first small component. String 3A; pass through the inside hole of the D just exited (**FIG. 4, RED THREAD**). Repeat the entire link thread path to reinforce. Secure this thread and trim.

FIG. 1: Forming Round 1 and adding the center of the small component

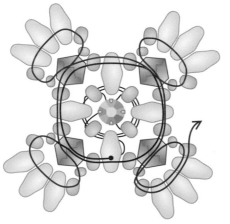

FIG. 2: Stitching Rounds 2 and 3 of the small component

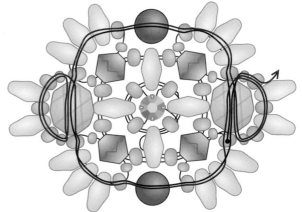

FIG. 3: Adding Rounds 4 and 5 of the small component

LINKS 2–4: Repeat Link 1 to connect all the components in this order: 2 small components, the large component, and 2 small components, taking care that the G are all on the same side of the bracelet. *NOTE: When the bracelet is laid out horizontally, connect the small components with the F in the east and west positions; connect the large component with the F in the north and south positions.*

4 Clasp

Use the working thread of the left-end small component (or start 2' [0.6 m] of new thread if needed) to string 3A; pass through the outside hole of the nearest D. String 2B, 1 loop of one half of the clasp, and 2B; pass through the same hole just exited to form a loop (**FIG. 5, GREEN THREAD**). *NOTE: Be sure that the front of the clasp and the G are both on the front of the bracelet.* Repeat the thread path to reinforce. Pass through the inside hole of the same D. Continue through 1C, 1B, 1F, 1B, and 1C (**FIG. 5, BLUE THREAD**). String 3A; pass through the outside hole of the nearest D. String 2B, the second loop of the clasp, and 2B; pass through the same hole just exited to form a loop (**FIG. 5, RED THREAD**). Repeat the thread path to reinforce. Secure the thread and trim. Repeat this entire step on the other end of the bracelet to add the other half of the clasp, taking care that it is positioned properly to connect to the first half of the clasp.

Artist's Tips

- Reinforcing the links is very important.

- To change the look of this bracelet, try substituting 4mm fire-polished rounds for the 4mm pressed-glass rounds. You may also substitute 6mm pressed-glass rounds for the 6mm fire-polished rounds.

- A 3mm pearl bead at the center of the components is a lovely substitute for the 3mm rose montée.

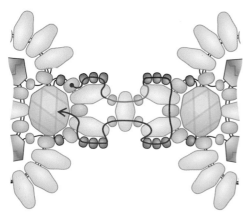

FIG. 4: Linking 2 small components

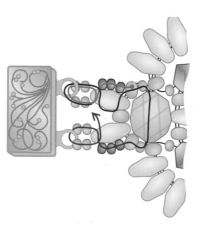

FIG. 5: Adding the clasp

Lacy Cables

Barbara Falkowitz

techniques
Right-angle weave variation

Picot

Netting

materials
2 g metallic antique bronze size 15° seed beads (A)

1 g silver-lined aqua size 15° seed beads (B)

4 g metallic antique bronze size 11° seed beads (C)

7 g turquoise Picasso 4×2mm 2-hole MiniDuos (D)

55 rose gold luster opaque 4mm fire-polished rounds (E)

36 crystal Picasso 3mm pressed-glass rounds (F)

1 antiqued copper 22mm 3-strand box clasp

Smoke 6 lb FireLine braided beading thread

tools
Scissors

Size 10 beading needle

finished size
6¾" (17 cm)

① Base

Use a variation of right-angle weave to stitch the base:

ROW 1, UNIT 1: Use 3' (0.9 m) of thread to string {1D and 1C} four times, leaving a 4" (10 cm) tail. Pass through the beads (same holes of the D) again to form a tight circle; use the working and tail threads to tie a square knot and pass through the first (inside) hole of the first D strung. Pass through the second (outside) hole of the last D exited (**FIG. 1, GREEN THREAD**).

ROW 1, UNIT 2: String {1C and 1D} three times. String 1C; pass through the last D (outside hole) exited in the previous unit and the first 1C, 1D (inside hole), 1C, and 1D (inside then outside holes) of this unit (**FIG. 1, BLUE THREAD**).

ROW 1, UNITS 3-19: Repeat Row 1, Unit 2 seventeen times, exiting toward the beadwork from the first D (inside then outside holes) of Row 1, Unit 19 (**FIG. 1, RED THREAD**).

ROW 2, UNIT 1: String {1C and 1D} three times. String 1C; pass through the last D (outside hole) exited in the previous row and the first 1C/1D (inside then outside holes) of this unit (**FIG. 2, GREEN THREAD**).

ROW 2, UNIT 2: String 1C; pass through the D (outside hole) at the bottom of the next unit in the previous row. String {1C and 1D} twice. String 1C; pass through the last D (outside hole) exited in the previous unit of the current row, and weave through beads to exit from the first D (inside then outside holes) of this unit (**FIG. 2, BLUE THREAD**).

ROW 2, UNITS 3-19: Repeat Row 2, Unit 2 seventeen times, exiting away from the beadwork from the second D (inside then outside holes) of Row 2, Unit 19 (**FIG. 2, RED THREAD**).

ROW 3, UNIT 1: String {1C and 1D} three times. String 1C; pass through the last D (outside hole) exited in the previous row and weave through beads to exit from the third D (inside then outside holes) of this unit (**FIG. 3, GREEN THREAD**).

ROW 3, UNIT 2: String {1C and 1D} twice. String 1C; pass through the D (outside hole) at the bottom of the next unit in the previous row. String 1C; pass through the last D (outside hole) exited in the previous unit of the current row, and weave through beads to exit from the second D (inside then outside holes) of this unit (**FIG. 3, BLUE THREAD**).

ROW 3, UNITS 3-19: Repeat Row 3, Unit 2 seventeen times, exiting away from the beadwork from the first D (inside hole) of Row 3, Unit 19 (**FIG. 3, RED THREAD**).

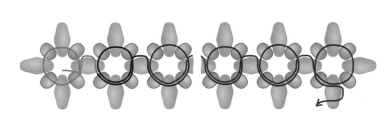

FIG. 1: Stitching Row 1 of the base

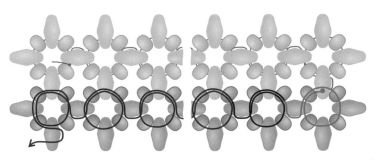

FIG. 2: Working Row 2 of the base

Artist's Tip

- Keep consistent tension when stitching the base.

② Edge 1, Row 1

Use picots and netting to embellish one edge of the base:

END 1: String 2A; pass through the last D (outside hole) exited (**FIG. 4, BLACK THREAD**).

STITCH 1: String 3A; pass through the last D (outside hole) exited (**FIG. 4, PINK THREAD**).

STITCH 2: String 1A, 1E, and 1A; pass through the next edge D (outside hole) (**FIG. 4, TURQUOISE THREAD**).

STITCHES 3–37: Repeat Stitches 1 and 2 seventeen times. Repeat Stitch 1 (**FIG. 4, PURPLE THREAD**).

END 2: String 2A; pass back through the nearest C and the next 1D (inside hole), 1C, and 1D (inside hole) (**FIG. 4, GREEN THREAD**).

③ Edge 1, Row 2

String 3A and pass through the last D (inside hole) exited, then weave through beads to exit from the next D (inside hole) of the current row; repeat seventeen times (**FIG. 4, BLUE THREAD**). String 3A; pass through the last D (inside hole) exited and the first 2A of the last 3A added (**FIG. 4, RED THREAD**).

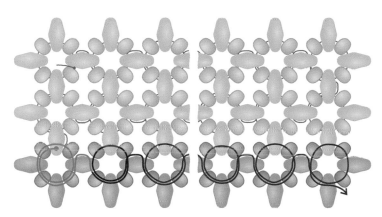

FIG. 3: Forming Row 3 of the base

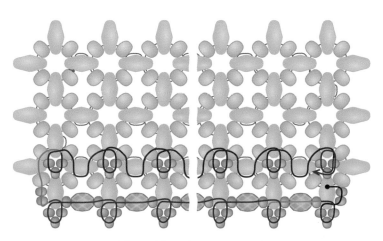

FIG. 4: Adding Edge 1, Rows 1 and 2

MAIN COLORWAY

4 Edge 1, Row 3

String 1B, 1C, 1F, 1C, and 1B and pass through the second A of the next 3A set in Edge 1, Row 2 (**FIG. 5, ORANGE THREAD**); repeat seventeen times. Weave through beads to exit from the second A of the nearest 3A set in Edge 1, Row 1 (**FIG. 5, PURPLE THREAD**).

5 Edge 1, Row 4

String 1B and 1C and pass back through the nearest F of Edge 1, Row 3, then string 1C and 1B and pass through the second A of the next 3A set in Edge 1, Row 1 (**FIG. 5, GREEN THREAD**); repeat seventeen times (**FIG. 5, BLUE THREAD**). Weave through beads to exit from the mirror D (inside hole) at the other edge of the base, away from the beadwork (**FIG. 5, RED THREAD**).

6 Edge 2, Rows 1–4

Repeat Steps 2–5. Weave through beads to exit from one end C of Row 2 in the base (see the blue start dot in **FIG. 6**).

7 Centerline

String 1A, 1E, and 1A and pass through the diagonal C of the current unit in Row 2 of the base, then weave through beads to exit from the mirror C of the next unit in Row 2 of the base (**FIG. 6, BLUE THREAD**); repeat eighteen times (**FIG. 6, RED THREAD**). Secure the threads and trim.

8 Clasp

Start 2' (0.6 m) of new thread that exits from one end D (outside hole) of Row 1 in the base, away from the beadwork, leaving a 4" (10 cm) tail. *String 3A, the end loop of one half of the clasp, and 3A, then pass through the last D (outside hole) exited; repeat the thread path of the 3A/clasp loop/3A to reinforce. Weave through beads to exit from the next D (outside hole) at the end of the base (**FIG. 7, GREEN THREAD**). Repeat from *, stringing the next loop of the same half of the clasp (**FIG. 7, BLUE THREAD**). String 3A, the last loop of the same half of the clasp, and 3A; pass through the last D (outside hole) exited (**FIG. 7, RED THREAD**). Secure the threads and trim.

Repeat this entire step at the other end of the bracelet, using the second half of the clasp and taking care that the clasp is positioned to close properly.

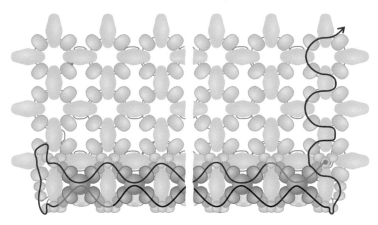

FIG. 5: Working Edge 1, Rows 3 and 4

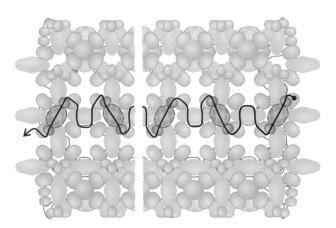

FIG. 6: Stitching the centerline

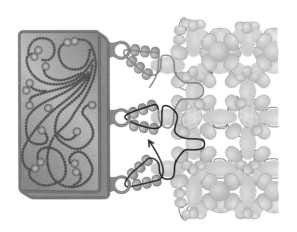

FIG. 7: Attaching the clasp

variations

- Use 2mm fire-polished rounds, 2×3mm crystal rondelles, or 3mm pearls for the 3mm pressed-glass rounds.

- Use one color of size 15° seed beads instead of two.

alternate colorway materials

4 g teal purple iris size 15° seed beads (Use for A and B.)

4 g wisteria luster size 11° seed beads (C)

7 g turquoise blue bronze Picasso 4×2mm 2-hole MiniDuos (D)

49 amethyst opal luster 4mm fire-polished rounds (E)

32 bordeaux pastel 2mm fire-polished rounds (F)

1 silver 22mm 3-strand box clasp

Smoke 6 lb FireLine braided beading thread

This variation has 17 units in each base row.

finished size

6¼" (16 cm)

ALTERNATE COLORWAY

Botanic Gardens

Svetlana Chernitsky

techniques

Netting

Fringe

materials

2 g metallic gold iris size 15° seed beads (A)

5 g turquoise Picasso size 11° seed beads (B)

2 g metallic gold iris size 8° seed beads (C)

7 g turquoise Picasso 5×2.5mm 2-hole seed beads (D)

7 g light blue opaque brown luster 5×2.5mm 2-hole seed beads (E)

3 g matte metallic copper 5×2.5mm 2-hole seed beads (F)

42 umber 6×3mm 2-hole brick beads (G)

1 antiqued brass 16×19mm toggle clasp

3 antiqued brass 6mm jump rings

Smoke 6 lb braided beading thread

tools

Scissors

Size 12 beading needle

2 pairs of chain- or flat-nose pliers

finished size

7" (18 cm)

① Base

Use netting to form the body of the bracelet:

ROW 1, PASS 1: Add a stop bead to 6' (1.8 m) of thread, leaving an 8" (20.5 cm) tail. String 1G, 2B, 1A, 1D, 2A, 1B, 2A; pass through the second hole of the D just added. String 1A, 3B, 1A, 1D, 2A, 1B, 2A; pass through the second hole of the last D added. String 1A, 2B, and 1G; pass through the second hole of the last G added (**FIG. 1, BLUE THREAD**).

ROW 1, PASS 2: String 1E and 1B; pass down through the nearest A of Pass 1, through the nearest hole of the D, and the next A. String 1A, 1B, and 1A; pass up through the nearest A of Pass 1, through the nearest hole of the D, and the next A. String 1B, 1F, and 1B; pass down through the next 1A/1D/1A of Pass 1. String 1A, 1B, and 1A; pass up through the next 1A/1D/1A of Pass 1. String 1B and 1E; pass through the second hole of the first G of Pass 1 (**FIG. 1, RED THREAD**).

ROW 2, PASS 1: String 1E, 1B, 1C, and 1B; pass through the second hole of the E just added. String 1G and pass through the second hole of the last E in the previous row. String 1B, 1A, 1D, 2A, 1B, and 2A; pass through the second hole of the D just added. String 1A and 1B; pass through the second hole of the F in the previous row. String 1B, 1A, 1D, 2A, 1B, and 2A; pass through the second hole of the D just added. String 1A and 1B; pass through the second hole of the next E in the previous row. String 1G; pass through the second hole of the same G (**FIG. 2, BLUE THREAD**).

ROW 2, PASS 2: String 1E and 1B; pass down through the nearest 1A/1D/1A of the previous pass. String 1A; pass back through the nearest B of the previous row. String 1A; pass up through the nearest 1A/1D/1A of the previous pass. String 1B, 1F, and 1B; pass down through the next 1A/1D/1A of the previous pass. String 1A; pass back through the nearest B of the previous row. String 1A; pass up through the next 1A/1D/1A of the previous

pass. String 1B and 1E; pass through the second hole of the first G in this row (**FIG. 2, RED THREAD**).

ROWS 3–20: Repeat Row 2, Passes 1 and 2, eighteen times or to the desired length minus 1¼" (3.2 cm) for Row 21 and the clasp.

ROW 21, PASS 1: Repeat Row 2, Pass 1, but string 2A before passing through the second hole of the final G (**FIG. 3, GREEN THREAD**).

ROW 21, PASS 2: String 2B; pass down through the nearest 1A/1D/1A of the previous pass. String 1A; pass back through the nearest B of the previous row. String 1A; pass up through the next 1A/1D/1A of the previous pass. String 3B; pass down through the next 1A/1D/1A of the previous pass. String 1A; pass back through the nearest B of the previous row. String 1A; pass up through the next 1A/1D/1A of the previous pass. String 2B; pass through the second hole of the first G in this row (**FIG. 3, BLUE THREAD**).

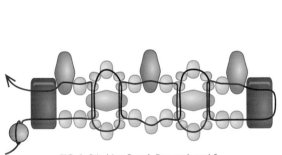

FIG. 1: Stitching Row 1, Passes 1 and 2

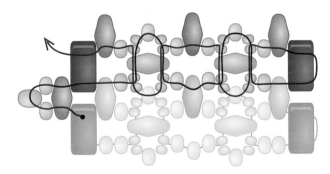

FIG. 2: Adding Row 2, Passes 1 and 2

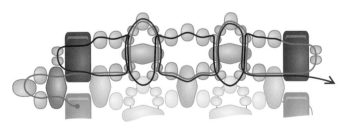

FIG. 3: Working Row 21, Passes 1 and 2

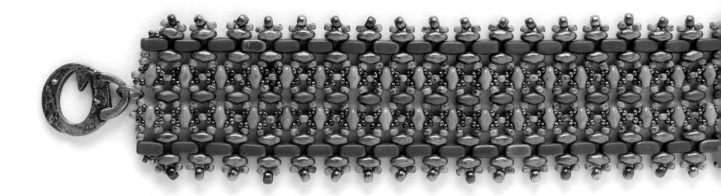

String 2A; pass through the first (bottom) hole of the last G exited. Weave through beads to exit from the bottom hole of the G on the other side of this row (**FIG. 3, RED THREAD**). Repeat the thread path to reinforce, exiting from the bottom hole of the G. Remove the stop bead.

② Edge Embellishment

Add fringe to the bracelet edge:

FRINGE: Turn the work so that the smooth, long edge of the bracelet points up.

String 1E, 1B, 1C, and 1B, then pass through the second hole of the E just added, down through the next G along the edge of the bracelet, and up through the next hole of the same G; repeat nineteen times to embellish this edge of the bracelet to match the other edge (**FIG. 4, GREEN THREAD**).

END: String 2A; pass down through the previous hole of the last G exited (**FIG. 4, BLUE THREAD**). Weave through beads, reinforcing the B at the end of the

bracelet, to exit from the mirror G on the other side of the bracelet. String 2A; pass up through the second hole of the same G (**FIG. 4, RED THREAD**). Secure the thread and trim.

③ Assembly

Use 1 jump ring to attach the ring half of the clasp to one end of the bracelet, connecting to the loop of B at the center. Attach 1 jump ring to the other end of the bracelet. Use 1 jump ring to attach the previous jump ring to the bar half of the clasp.

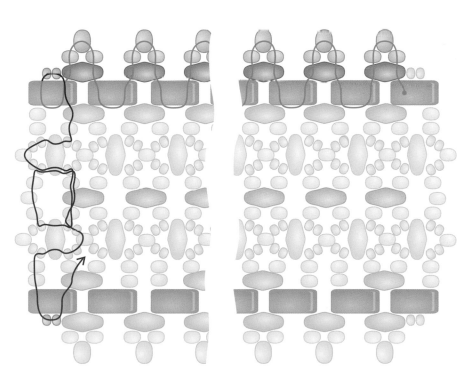

FIG. 4: Adding the edge embellishments

Crystal Waltz

Monique de Boer

techniques

Netting

Right-angle weave

materials

5 g nickel size 15° seed beads (A)

2 g galvanized peacock blue size 11° seed beads (B)

180 light gray 3mm glass pearls (C)

270 turquoise AB 2×3mm crystal bicones (D)

1 sterling silver 22×20mm 5-strand filigree box clasp

10 silver 5mm split rings

Crystal 4 lb braided beading thread

tools

Scissors

Size 12 beading needles

finished size

7" (18 cm)

① Row 1

Form netted circles and connect them with right-angle-weave links to create the first row of the bracelet band. *NOTE: It's best to pass through each round again to reinforce the beads.*

CIRCLE 1, ROUND 1: Use 8' (2.4 cm) of thread to string {1B and 1C} six times, leaving a 6" (15 cm) tail. Pass through the beads again to form a tight circle; exit from the first B.

CIRCLE 1, ROUND 2: String 5A and pass through the next B of Round 1; repeat five times for a total of 6 nets. Step up through the first 3A added in this round (**FIG. 1, GREEN THREAD**).

CIRCLE 1, ROUND 3: String 1D and pass through the third A of the next net in Round 2; repeat five times for a total of 6D. Step up through the first D added in this round (**FIG. 1, BLUE THREAD**).

CIRCLE 1, ROUND 4: Pass through the 6D of Round 3 and the 5A of Round 2, without adding beads, to cinch the beads at the top of the circle. Weave through beads to exit from a C of Round 1 (**FIG. 1, RED THREAD**). *NOTE: Always pull the thread in the direction the beads were strung, or the thread may break.*

LINK: String 1A, 1D, 1A, 1C, 1A, 1D, and 1A; pass through the last C of Round 1 exited. Weave through beads to exit from the C just added (**FIG. 2, BLUE THREAD**).

CIRCLE 2, ROUND 1: String {1B and 1C} five times; then string 1B and pass through the last C exited and the first B just added (**FIG. 2, RED THREAD**).

CIRCLE 2, ROUNDS 2–4: Repeat Circle 1, Rounds 2–4.

ROW 1 FINISH: Repeat the link and Circle 2 eight times for a total of 10 circles. Weave through beads to exit from the bottom D added in the last link, toward the center of the work. *NOTE: For a longer or shorter bracelet, stitch more or fewer circle repeats with links in between.*

② Row 2

Form the second row of the band:

LINK 1: String {1A and 1D} three times; then string 1A and pass through the last D exited in Row 1. Weave through the first A/D/A/D just added (**FIG. 3, GREEN THREAD**). String 1A, 1C, 1A, 1D, 1A, 1C, and 1A; pass through the last D exited and the first A/C just added (**FIG. 3, BLUE THREAD**).

CIRCLE 1, ROUND 1: String {1B and 1C} five times; then string 1B and pass through the last C exited in Link 1 and the first B just strung (**FIG. 3, RED THREAD**).

CIRCLE 1, ROUNDS 2–4: Repeat Circle 1, Rounds 2–4, of Row 1. Weave through beads to exit from the leftmost C of Link 1 in this step.

CIRCLE 2, ROUNDS 1–4: Repeat Circle 1 of this step. Weave through beads to exit from the leftmost C of Circle 2, Round 1.

LINK 2: String 1A, 1D, 1A, 1C, 1A, 1D, and 1A; pass through the last C exited in Circle 2, then weave through the beads again to reinforce. Exit from the top D of the circle just formed (**FIG. 4, GREEN THREAD**). String 1A, 1D, and 1A; pass through the bottom D of the nearest Row 1 link. String 1A, 1D, and 1A; pass through the last D exited in this link. Weave through beads to exit from the leftmost C of the link just formed (**FIG. 4, BLUE THREAD**).

CIRCLE 3, ROUND 1: String {1B and 1C} five times; then string 1B and pass through the last C exited and the first B just strung (**FIG. 4, RED THREAD**).

CIRCLE 3, ROUNDS 2–4: Repeat Circle 1, Rounds 2–4, of Row 1. Weave through beads to exit from the leftmost C of Round 1 in this circle.

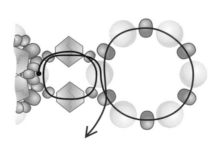

FIG. 1: Stitching Rounds 1–4 of Circle 1 in Row 1

FIG. 2: Adding the link and Round 1 of Circle 2 in Row 1

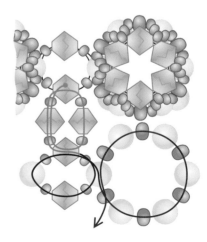

FIG. 3: Forming Link 1 and Round 1 of Circle 1 in Row 2

ROW 2 FINISH: Repeat Link 2 and Circle 3 of this step seven times for a total of 10 circles. Weave through beads to exit from the bottom D added in the last link, toward the center of the work.

③ Row 3

Repeat Row 2, forming 10 circles that are connected to each other and to Row 2 with the same type of links formed in Row 2. Secure the thread and trim. *NOTE: Because you will now be working from left to right, the direction of the thread path mirrors the one worked right to left, but the concept is the same.*

④ Clasp

Connect 1 split ring to each loop on one half of the clasp. Start 12" (30.5 cm) of new thread that exits from the top left B of Row 1, Circle 1, Round 1 at the end of the bracelet, toward the center of the beadwork. String 6A and the top ring of the clasp, taking care that the clasp's and band's tops are oriented correctly. Pass through the next B of Round 1 in this circle and back through the last A added. String 5A; pass through the nearest B of the end circle in Row 2 and back through the last A strung. String 5A; pass through the next B

of Round 1 in this circle and back through the last A added. String 5A; pass through the nearest B of the end circle in Row 3 and back through the last A strung. String 5A; pass through the next B of Round 1 in this circle (**FIG. 5**). Repeat the entire thread path to reinforce. Secure the thread and trim. Repeat this step to add the other half of the clasp to the other end of the bracelet.

Artist's Tips

- For a more delicate look, create a bracelet with just one row. For a bolder bracelet, stitch five rows.

- To make an extra-sparkly bracelet, add 8mm crystal chatons or rivolis to the center of the circles. Just be sure to place the crystal between Rounds 2 and 3 so it's safely captured by the bicones.

- Form matching earrings by stitching the circles only and adding an ear wire.

MAIN COLORWAY

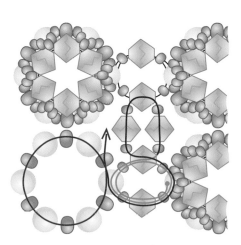

FIG. 4: Stitching Link 2 and Round 1 of Circle 3 in Row 2

FIG. 5: Adding the clasp

25

Clinging Vine

Cristie Prince

techniques

Spiral netting

Tubular peyote stitch

Picot

Fringe

Ladder stitch

materials

4 g gold-lined aqua size 15° seed beads (A)

6 g lavender 1.5mm cube beads (B)

12 tanzanite AB 3mm crystal bicones (C)

12 tanzanite AB 4mm crystal bicones (D)

2 tanzanite 6.5×13mm crystal briolettes

2 rounds of oval bracelet-sized memory wire

8" (20.5 cm) of clear 2mm plastic tubing

Smoke 4 lb braided beading thread

Talcum powder (optional)

tools

Memory-wire cutters

Scissors

Size 12 beading needle

Drinking straw

Flat-nose pliers

Round-nose pliers

finished size

Adjustable

① Base

Prepare the wire and tube to form the bracelet base:

WIRE: Cut a piece of memory wire to fit around the wrist plus a ½" (1.3 cm) overlap on each end (a 1" [2.5 cm] total overlap).

TUBING: Cut a length of tubing equal to the memory wire. Slide the memory wire inside the tubing. Use round-nose pliers to form a loop that curls up around the outside of one end of the tubing. Use flat-nose pliers to flatten the loop against the tubing (**FIG. 1**). *NOTE: If the tubing doesn't slide easily over the wire, cut the tubing into a few pieces and slide them on, or put some talcum powder on the wire first.* Don't finish the other end of the wire. Set the base aside.

② Rope

Stitch a spiral netted rope:

ROUND 1: Use 6' (1.8 m) of thread to string {1B and 2A} three times, leaving a 2' (0.6 m) tail. *NOTE: Each 1B and 2A set forms a net.* Tie a knot to form a tight circle and pass through the first 1B and 1A (**FIG. 2, BLUE THREAD**). Slide the circle onto the straw.

ROUNDS 2 AND ON: String 1B and 2A, then pass through the first A of the next net (**FIG. 2, RED THREAD**); repeat to the length of the memory wire. *NOTE: You'll know that the spiral is being stitched correctly if there are 3B along the top of the spiral; if there are only 2B, you've dropped a stitch.* Remove the straw.

③ Embellish

Finish and add fringe to one end of the rope:

PEYOTE-STITCHED ROUNDS: Place a needle on the tail and weave through beads to exit from a B of Round 1. *String 1B and pass through the next B of Round 1; repeat twice and step up through the first B added in this round. Repeat from * once.

DROP: String 1 briolette and pass through 1B on the other side of the final round. Pass back through the briolette and the original B (**FIG. 3**). Repeat the thread path several times to reinforce. Exit from 1B in the final round and work 3 tubular peyote stitches with 1B in each stitch (**FIG. 4, BLUE THREAD**). Weave through the 6B at the end of the rope to reinforce and tighten. Exit from the 1B just placed (**FIG. 4, RED THREAD**).

FIG. 1: Preparing the base

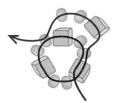

FIG. 2: Working the first stitch of Round 2 off of Round 1

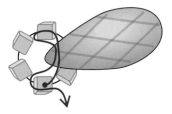

FIG. 3: Adding the briolette

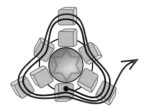

FIG. 4: Securing the briolette with peyote stitch

FIG. 5: Adding a small fringe

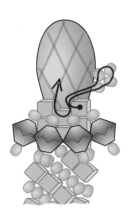

FIG. 6: Stitching a large picot

FIG. 7: Forming the first large fringe

FIG. 8: Adding a small picot

SMALL FRINGE: String 1A, 1C, and 1A; pass back through the C and first A to form a fringe, then pass through the nearest B at the end of the rope (**FIG. 5**). Repeat five times for a total of 6 small fringes.

LARGE PICOTS: Push the small fringes toward the body of the rope. String 4A, pass back through the first A just added, and pass through the nearest B to form a picot (**FIG. 6**); repeat five times for a total of 6 large picots.

LARGE FRINGE: Push the small fringes and picots toward the body of the rope. String 1A, 1D, and 3A; pass back through the D and the first A to form a fringe. Pass through the same B just exited to anchor the fringe and pass through the nearest B (**FIG. 7**). Repeat five times for a total of 6 large fringes.

SMALL PICOTS: Push the large fringes toward the drop and the small fringes and picots toward the body of the rope. String 3A, then pass through the last B exited and the nearest B (**FIG. 8**); repeat five times for a total of 6 small picots.

REINFORCE: Weave through beads to exit from the final rounds of netting. Work a ladder-stitch thread path to reinforce these rounds. Secure the thread and trim.

④ Finish

Carefully slide the base inside the rope, curled end first. Trim the wire as necessary on the unfinished end of the bracelet; loop and flatten it against the tubing as with the other end. Adjust the netting as necessary, adding or removing stitches to equal the length of the base. Repeat Step 3 to embellish the other end of the bracelet.

Artist's Tips

- You may substitute 1.8mm cubes for the 1.5mm ones.

- This design also makes a great lariat; just stitch the rope long enough to drape around your neck. Omit the memory wire/tubing base, add an extra round of peyote-stitched cubes, and add an extra round of large fringe.

- Sometimes it's easier to form the large fringe and a picot at the same time. Doing it in rounds is correct, too, so choose which way works best for you.

MAIN COLORWAY

Cactus Flower

Carole E. Hanley

techniques

Ladder stitch

Brick stitch

materials

4 g gold size 11° cylinder beads (A)

4 g royal blue size 11° cylinder beads (B)

1 g dark turquoise size 11° cylinder beads (C)

1 g turquoise size 11° cylinder beads (D)

1 g aqua size 11° cylinder beads (E)

1 g lime size 11° cylinder beads (F)

1 g yellow size 11° cylinder beads (G)

1 gold-plated 7×12mm lobster clasp

2" (5 cm) of gold-plated 3×4mm curb extension chain with charm

White size B Nymo nylon beading thread

tools

Scissors

Size 11 beading needle

finished size

7¼" (18.5 cm) (adjustable to 9" [23 cm])

① Band

Use ladder stitch and brick stitch to form the bracelet band:

ROW 1: Use 6' (1.8 m) of thread to string 2A; pass through the beads again and exit the first A strung, leaving a 6" (15 cm) tail (**FIG. 1**).

ROW 2 (INCREASE): String 1A and 1B; pass under the exposed thread loop between the 2A of Row 1, then pass back through the B just added (**FIG. 2, BLUE THREAD**). String 1A; pass under the same exposed thread loop and back through the last A added (**FIG. 2, RED THREAD**).

ROW 3 (INCREASE): String 1A and 1B; pass under the nearest exposed thread loop and back through the last B added. String 1B; pass under the next exposed thread loop and back through the last B added. String 1A; pass under the same exposed thread loop as in the previous stitch and back through the last A added (**FIG. 3, BLUE THREAD**).

ROW 4 (INCREASE): String 1A and 1B; pass under the nearest exposed thread loop and back through the last B added. String 1A; pass under the next exposed thread loop and back through the A just added. String 1B; pass under the next exposed thread loop and back through the last B added. String 1A; pass under the same exposed thread loop as in the previous stitch and back through the last A added (**FIG. 3, RED THREAD**).

ROWS 5–22 (INCREASES): Continue in brick stitch, following the pattern in **FIG. 4**, to form increases. *NOTE: The last 2 stitches of each row will be formed in the same exposed thread loop.*

FIG. 1: Working Row 1

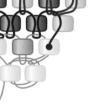

FIG. 2: Stitching Row 2

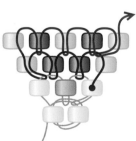

FIG. 3: Working Rows 3 and 4

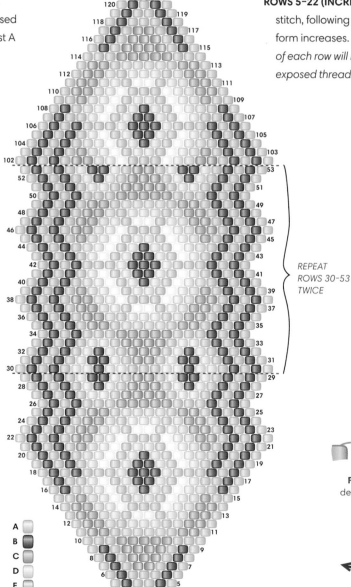

REPEAT ROWS 30–53 TWICE

A
B
C
D
E
F
G

FIG. 4: Brick-stitch pattern

FIG. 5: Forming a decrease at the start of Row 23

FIG. 6: Forming a decrease at the end of Row 23

ROWS 23–26 (DECREASES): String 1A and 1B; skip the nearest exposed thread loop and pass under the next exposed thread loop. Pass back through the B just added (**FIG. 5, BLUE THREAD**). Pass back through the first 2 beads of this row to make the edge bead sit flat against the previous row (**FIG. 5, RED THREAD**). Continue brick-stitching the row as before, adding 1 bead to each exposed thread loop and following the pattern in **FIG. 4**. *NOTE: The last 2 stitches of decrease rows aren't formed in the same exposed thread loop as when making increases (**FIG. 6**).*

ROWS 27–53: Continue in brick stitch, following the pattern in **FIG. 4**, to form increases and decreases. When working increase rows, follow the thread path of Rows 3 and 4; when working decrease rows, follow the thread path of Row 23.

ROWS 54–101: Repeat Rows 30–53 twice. Repeat Rows 30–23 (working backward by stitching Row 30, then Row 29, etc.)

ROWS 102–123 (DECREASES): Continue in brick stitch, following the pattern in **FIG. 4**, to form decreases.

② Clasp

String the ring of the clasp and pass through the 2A of Row 123; repeat the thread path several times to reinforce. Secure the working thread and trim. Using the tail thread, repeat this entire step to attach the end of the chain that's opposite the charm to Row 1.

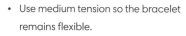

MAIN COLORWAY

ALTERNATE COLORWAY

Artist's Tips

- Use medium tension so the bracelet remains flexible.

- Main colorway of bracelet shown uses the following Delica color numbers: DB42 for A, DB726 for B, DB918 for C, DB658 for D, DB79 for E, DB733 for F, and DB721 for G.

Dancing Diamonds

Carole E. Hanley

techniques

Ladder stitch

Brick stitch

materials

2 g tarnished silver galvanized size 11° cylinder beads (A)

2 g opaque Ceylon cream size 11° cylinder beads (B)

2 g opaque turquoise green size 11° cylinder beads (C)

1 g opaque dark blue size 11° cylinder beads (D)

1 g silver-lined gold size 11° cylinder beads (F)

1 gunmetal 6×12mm lobster clasp with attached 4mm soldered jump ring

1 gunmetal 6mm jump ring

2" (5 cm) of gunmetal 3.5×5mm soldered curb chain

Cream size B nylon beading thread

tools

Scissors

Size 11 beading needle

2 pairs of chain- or flat-nose pliers

finished size

6½" (16.5 cm) (adjustable to 9½" [24 cm])

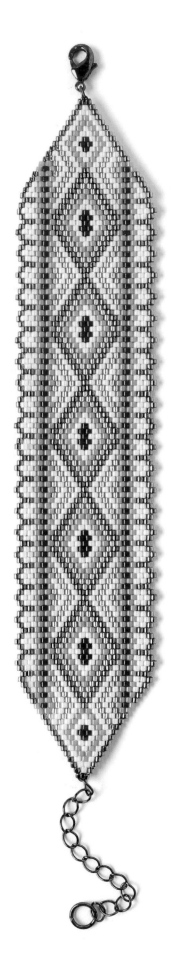

① Band

Use ladder stitch and brick stitch to form the bracelet band:

ROW 1: Use 6' (1.8 m) of thread to string 2A; pass through the beads again and exit the first A strung, leaving a 6" (15 cm) tail (**FIG. 1**).

ROW 2 (INCREASE): String 1A and 1B; pass under the exposed thread loop between the 2A of Row 1, then pass back through the B just added (**FIG. 2, BLUE THREAD**). String 1A; pass under the same exposed thread loop and back through the last A added (**FIG. 2, RED THREAD**).

ROW 3 (INCREASE): String 1A and 1B; pass under the nearest exposed thread loop and back through the last B added. String 1B; pass under the next exposed thread loop and back through the last B added. String 1A; pass under the same exposed thread loop as in the previous stitch and back through the last A added (**FIG. 3, BLUE THREAD**).

ROW 4 (INCREASE): String 1A and 1B; pass under the nearest exposed thread loop and back through the last B added. String 1C; pass under the next exposed thread loop and back through the C just added. String 1B; pass under the next exposed thread loop and back through the last B added. String 1A; pass under the same exposed thread loop as in the previous stitch and back through the last A added (**FIG. 3, RED THREAD**).

ROWS 5–19 (INCREASES): Continue in brick stitch, following the pattern in **FIG. 4**, to form increases. *NOTE: The last 2 stitches of each row will be formed in the same exposed thread loop.*

ROW 20 (DECREASE): String 2A; skip the nearest exposed thread loop and pass under the next exposed thread loop. Pass back through the last A added (**FIG. 5, BLUE THREAD**). Pass back through the first 2A of this row to make the edge bead sit flat against the previous row (**FIG. 5, RED THREAD**).

Artist's Tips

- Use tension so the bracelet remains flexible.

- A light-colored thread is recommended for the body of the bracelet. If the thread shows too much where it is stitched around the chain and clasp, use a permanent marker to color the thread to match the end beads.

- Main colorway of bracelet shown uses the following Delica color numbers: #254 for A, #203 for B, #658 for C, #726 for D, and #42 for E.

Continue brick-stitching the row as before, adding 1 bead to each exposed thread loop and following the pattern in **FIG. 4**. *NOTE: The last 2 stitches of decrease rows are not formed in the same exposed thread loop as when making increases* (**FIG. 6**).

ROWS 21–44: Continue in brick stitch, following the pattern in **FIG. 4**. When working increase rows, follow the thread path of Row 4; when working decrease rows, follow the thread path of Row 20.

ROWS 45–104: Repeat Rows 25–44 three times.

ROWS 105–109: Continue in brick stitch, following the pattern in **FIG. 4**, to form increases and decreases.

ROWS 110–127 (DECREASES): Continue in brick stitch, following the pattern in **FIG. 4**, to form decreases.

2 Clasp

String the ring of the clasp and pass through the 2A of Row 127; repeat the thread path several times to reinforce. Secure the working thread and trim. Using the tail thread, repeat this entire step to attach one end of the chain to Row 1. Add the 6mm jump ring to the open end of the chain.

FIG. 1: Working Row 1

FIG. 2: Stitching Row 2

FIG. 3: Working Rows 3 and 4

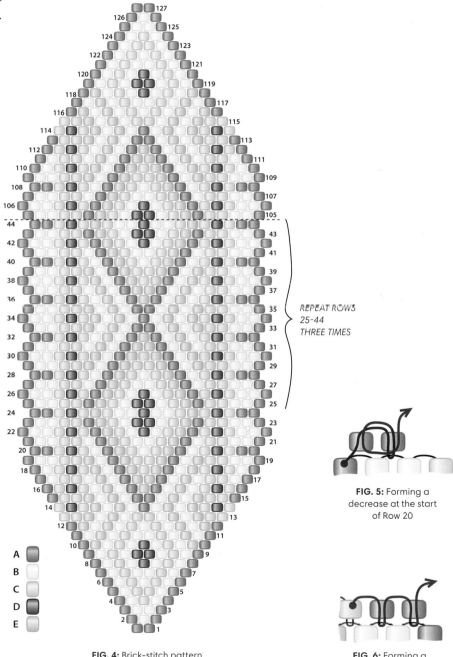

A
B
C
D
E

REPEAT ROWS 25–44 THREE TIMES

FIG. 4: Brick-stitch pattern

FIG. 5: Forming a decrease at the start of Row 20

FIG. 6: Forming a decrease at the end of Row 20

Dragon Dance

Csilla Csirmaz

techniques

Ladder stitch

Herringbone stitch

Peyote stitch

materials

1 g green iris size 15° seed beads (A)

1 g yellow-lined amber size 15° seed beads (B)

1 g metallic iris olivine size 15° seed beads (C)

1 g transparent golden olive luster size 11° seed beads (D)

2 g silver-lined ruby AB size 11° seed beads (E)

2 g matte metallic olive/purple iris size 8° hex-cut seed beads (F)

5 g matte dark olive 3mm cube beads (G)

18 wine 6–7mm cultured freshwater potato pearls (H)

1 gold-plated pewter 10×35mm hook-and-eye clasp

Smoke 6 lb braided beading thread

tools

Scissors

Size 10 beading needle

finished size

6⅜" (16.5 cm)

①Base

Use ladder and herringbone stitch to form the bracelet base:

ROW 1: String 1G, 1E, 1D, and 1F; pass through all the beads again, exiting up through the F. String 1E; pass up through the last F and down through the E. String 1B and 1C; pass down through the E and through the B/C (**FIG. 1**).

ROW 2: String 1C and 1E; pass down through the E of the previous row and up through the nearest F. String 1F and 1G; pass down through the next G of the previous row, loop the thread between beads to form a turnaround, and pass up through the nearest 2G (**FIG. 2**).

ROW 3: String 1G and 1F; pass down through the F of the previous row and up through the next E. String 1E and 1C; pass down through the next C of the previous row, string 1B, and pass up through the C just added (**FIG. 3, BLUE THREAD**).

ROW 4: String 1C and 1E; pass down through the E of the previous row and up through the next F. String 1F and 1G; pass down through the next G of the previous row, string 1D and 1E, and pass up through the G just added (**FIG. 3, RED THREAD**).

ROWS 5–14: Repeat Rows 3 and 4 five times to form a total of 14 rows. *NOTE: This completes one-half of a wave.*

ROW 15: String 1C and 1E; pass down through the F of the previous row and up through the next E. String 1F and 1G; pass down through the next C of the previous row, string 1B, and pass up through the G just added (**FIG. 4**).

ROWS 16–25: Repeat Rows 3 and 4 five times. *NOTE: This completes one full wave.*

ROWS 26–49: Repeat Row 15. Repeat Rows 3 and 4 six times, then repeat Rows 15–25.

ROWS 50–73: Repeat Row 15. Repeat Rows 3 and 4 six times, then repeat Rows 15–25.

Repeat Rows 3 and 4. Exit up through the final G. Work a final herringbone row with 1E and 1D in the first stitch and 1B in the second stitch so the ends of the bracelet match. Secure the thread and trim.

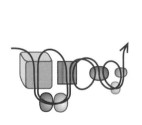

FIG. 1: Stitching Row 1

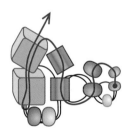

FIG. 2: Adding Row 2

FIG. 3: Forming Rows 3 and 4

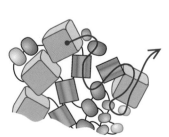

FIG. 4: Stitching Row 15

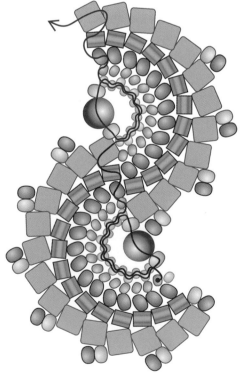

FIG. 5: Adding the inner pearls

② Inner Pearls

Start 3' (0.9 m) of new thread that exits down through the C of Row 1. *String 1A and pass through the next B along the edge of the base; repeat six times for a total of 7A. String 1D, 1H, and 1D; pass up through the series of A/B just exited and weave through beads to exit up through the last G added on the other side of the base on the current wave (**FIG. 5, BLUE THREAD**). Repeat from * five times for a total of 6H (except for the second through fifth half waves, only peyote-stitch 6A around the H) (**FIG. 5, RED THREAD**). Weave through beads to exit from the third-to-last D added along the outer edge of the base, toward the bracelet's end.

③ Clasp

String 7C and one-half of the clasp; pass back through the next E/D along the edge of the base. Repeat the thread path several times to reinforce. Weave through beads to exit from the final F added to the end of the base (**FIG. 6, BLUE THREAD**).

④ Outer Pearls

*String 2H; pass through the second G in the next full wave so that the 2H sit over the nearest H added in Step 2. Weave through beads to exit from the second-to-last G added to this half wave (**FIG. 6, RED THREAD**). Repeat from * twice. Weave through beads to exit from the other end of the base to add the other half of the clasp as in Step 3, then connect the waves on the other half of the bracelet as at the beginning of this step. Secure the thread and trim.

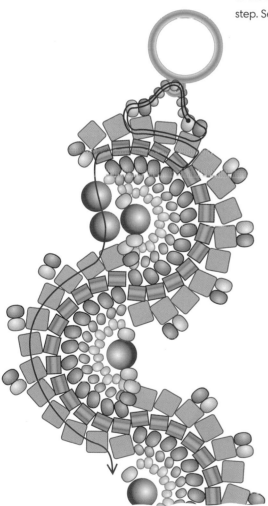

FIG. 6: Adding the clasp and outer pearls

Artist's Tips

- You can change the look of the bracelet by substituting crystal, pressed glass, or any type of round beads for the pearls.

- Make matching earrings by stitching one full wave and adding an ear wire to the loop at one end.

Dakota Canyon

Shae Wilhite

techniques

Peyote stitch

Brick stitch

materials

2 g pale seafoam frosted size 11° seed beads (A)

11 g brown-and-tan Picasso size 8° seed beads (B)

9 g champagne luster 5×2.5mm 2-hole SuperDuos (C)

9 g turquoise-green Picasso 5×2.5mm 2-hole SuperDuos (D)

6 g crystal bronze copper 5×2.5mm 2-hole SuperDuos (E)

1 antiqued copper 43×17mm magnetic glue-in bar clasp

Smoke 6 lb FireLine braided beading thread

Clear craft adhesive

tools

Scissors

Size 10 beading needle

finished size

7¾" (19.5 cm)

1 Base

Use peyote stitch to form the base of the bracelet:

BASE ROWS 1 AND 2: Add a stop bead to 6' (1.8 m) of thread, leaving a 12" (30.5 cm) tail. String 84B (**FIG. 1, BLUE THREAD**).

BASE ROW 3: String 1B, skip 1B of the previous row, and pass back through the next B of the previous row; repeat forty-one times (**FIG. 1, RED THREAD**).

BASE ROW 4: String 1B and pass back through the next B of the previous row; repeat forty-one times (**FIG. 2, BLUE THREAD**).

BASE ROW 5: Repeat Base Row 4 (**FIG. 2, RED THREAD**).

BASE ROW 6: Work 2 peyote stitches using 1C in each stitch. *NOTE: Continue working all peyote stitches with 1 bead in each stitch.* Work 3 peyote stitches using 1D, 1E, and 1D. Work 35 peyote stitches, repeating the following pattern five times: 4C, 1D, 1E, and 1D. Work 2 peyote stitches using 1C (**FIG. 3, GREEN THREAD**).

BASE ROW 7: String 1C and pass through the unused (second) hole of the next C in the previous row; repeat. *NOTE: When adding beads to a row made with SuperDuos, always pass through the second hole of the nearest previously added SuperDuo.* Work 4 peyote stitches using 1D, 2E, and 1D. Work 35 peyote stitches, repeating the following pattern five times: 3C, 1D, 2E, and 1D. Work 1 peyote stitch using 1C (**FIG. 3, BLUE THREAD**).

BASE ROW 8: String 1C and pass through the next C. Work 5 peyote stitches using 1D, 1E, 1D, 1E, and 1D. Work 35 peyote stitches, repeating the following pattern five times: 2C, 1D, 1E, 1D, 1E, and 1D. Work 1 peyote stitch using 1C (**FIG. 3, RED THREAD**).

BASE ROW 9: Work 42 peyote stitches, repeating the following pattern six times: 1C, 1D, 1E, 2D, 1E, and 1D.

BASE ROW 10: Work 42 peyote stitches, repeating the following pattern six times: 1D, 1E, 1D, 1C, 1D, 1E, and 1D.

BASE ROW 11: Work 42 peyote stitches, repeating the following pattern six times: 1D, 1E, 1D, 2C, 1D, and 1E.

BASE ROW 12: Work 42 peyote stitches, repeating the following pattern six times: 1E, 1D, 3C, 1D, and 1E.

BASE ROW 13: Work 42 peyote stitches, repeating the following pattern six times: 1E, 1D, 4C, and 1D.

BASE ROW 14: Work 42 peyote stitches with 1B in each stitch (**FIG. 4, GREEN THREAD**).

BASE ROWS 15–18: Repeat Base Row 4 four times (**FIG. 4, BLUE THREAD**).

BASE ROW 19: Work 42 peyote stitches with 1A in each stitch (**FIG. 4, RED THREAD**). Secure the working thread and trim.

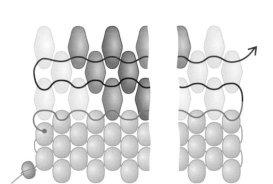

FIG. 1: Stitching Base Rows 1–3

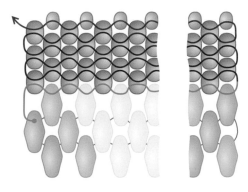

FIG. 2: Adding Base Rows 4 and 5

FIG. 3: Working Base Rows 6–8

FIG. 4: Stitching Base Rows 14–19

BASE ROW 20: Remove the stop bead. Use the tail thread to repeat Base Row 19, working off of Base Row 1. Secure the tail thread and trim.

2 Ends

Use brick stitch to add rows on both ends of the base that will be used to attach the clasp:

END 1, ROW 1: Start 3' (0.9 m) of new thread that exits from 1 end B of Base Row 1, leaving a 4" (10 cm) tail. String 2A; pass under the nearest exposed thread loop between beads at this end of the base and back up through the second A just strung (**FIG. 5, GREEN THREAD**). String 1A and pass under the nearest exposed thread loop on this end of the base and back through the A just added; repeat eleven times for a total of 14A (**FIG. 5, BLUE THREAD**). *NOTE: You'll pass through some exposed thread loops more than once.*

END 1, ROW 2: String 2A; pass under the nearest exposed thread loop between beads of End 1, Row 1 and back through the second A just added. String 1A and pass under the nearest exposed thread loop between beads of End 1, Row 1 and back through the A just added; repeat eleven times for a total of 14A (**FIG. 5, RED THREAD**). Secure the threads and trim.

END 2: Repeat End 1, Rows 1 and 2 on the other end of the bracelet.

3 Clasp

Use adhesive to coat the inside of one half of the clasp and the beads of one end from Step 2; insert the glued end into the clasp. Let dry.

Repeat this step on the other end of the bracelet, using the other half of the clasp and taking care that the clasp is positioned to close properly.

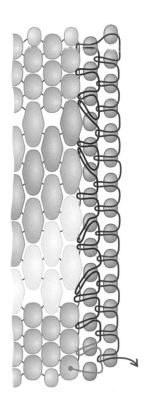

FIG. 5: Adding End 1

Artist's Tip

- Before stringing a SuperDuo, check both holes. Some bead finishes can block the holes, and it's easier to check before stringing than to undo a whole row of work.

28

Himalaya

Glenda Paunonen and Liisa Turunen

techniques
Circular, tubular, and flat peyote stitches

Picot

Fringe

materials
6 g metallic silver size 15° seed beads (A)

3 g platinum gray-blue size 11° cylinder beads (B)

5 g metallic steel blue size 11° seed beads (C)

5 g blue-lined clear size 8° seed beads (D)

10 white opal AB 2×3mm crystal bicones (E)

38 light gray 3mm crystal pearl rounds (F)

9 light blue 6mm crystal pearl rounds (G)

Light blue size B nylon beading thread

tools
Scissors

Size 10 or 12 beading needles

finished size
7" (18 cm)

1 Components

Use peyote stitch to form individual seed bead-and-pearl components:

ROUNDS 1 AND 2: Use 3' (0.9 m) of thread to string 1G and 8A, leaving a 6" (15 cm) tail; pass through the G so the 8A snug the G (**FIG. 1, BLUE THREAD**). String 8A; pass through the G to allow the 8A just added to snug the other side of the G, then pass through the original 8A (**FIG. 1, RED THREAD**). String 2A, pass through the last 8A added in this round, string 2A, and pass through the first 8A added. Pass through the following 3A (**FIG. 2**).

ROUNDS 3–5: String 1A, skip 1A of the previous round, and pass through the next 1A; repeat nine times for a total of 10A. Step up through the first A of this round. Repeat this entire step twice. Weave through beads to exit from 1A of Round 2 (**FIG. 3, BLUE THREAD**).

ROUND 6: Stitching off of Round 2, work 10 stitches with 1B in each stitch. Step up through the first B of this round (**FIG. 3, RED THREAD**).

ROUND 7: Turn the work so the thread exits from the top of the beadwork. Work 1 stitch with 1F and 4 stitches with 1C in each stitch; repeat. Step up through the first F of this round (**FIG. 4, BLUE THREAD**).

ROUND 8: Work 2 stitches with 1C in each stitch and 1 stitch with 1D, then work 2 stitches with 1C in each stitch; repeat. Step up through the first C of this round (**FIG. 4, RED THREAD**).

ROUND 9: Work 1 stitch with 3A, 2 stitches with 1D in each stitch, 1 stitch with 3A, and 1 stitch with 1C, 1F, and 1C; repeat. Weave through beads to exit from the first D of this round (**FIG. 5**). Don't cut the working thread; secure and trim the tail thread. Set aside.

Repeat this entire step eight times for a total of 9 components.

2 Link

Stitch the components together with seed beads and crystals:

STITCH 1: Use the working thread of 1 component to string 1D; pass through the next D of Round 9 in the same component. Then pass up through the third D of Round 9 in another component, back through the last D

FIG. 1: Forming the component, Rounds 1 and 2

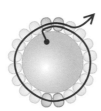

FIG. 2: Filling in the ends of the component, Rounds 1 and 2

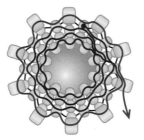

FIG. 3: Adding the component's Rounds 3–6

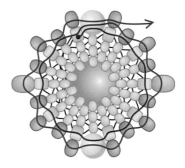

FIG. 4: Stitching the component's Rounds 7 and 8

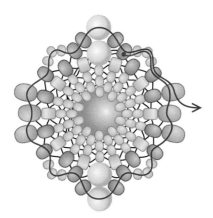

FIG. 5: Working the component's Round 9

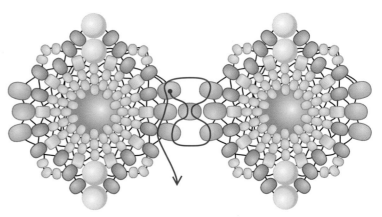

FIG. 6: Forming the link, Stitch 1

added, through the next D of the second component, down through the first D exited in the first component, and through the nearest D of Round 8 in the first component (**FIG. 6**).

STITCH 2: String 1A, 1E, and 1A; pass through the mirror D of Round 8 in the second component. String 1A; pass back through the last E added. String 1A; pass through the first D exited in this stitch and the following D of Round 9 of the first component (**FIG. 7, BLUE THREAD**).

STITCH 3: String 1A, 1C, and 1A; pass up through the mirror D of Round 9 in the second component, the following D of Round 8, and the next D of Round 9. String 1A, 1C, and 1A; pass down

through the mirror D of Round 9 in the first component (**FIG. 7, RED THREAD**). Secure the thread and trim.

Repeat this entire step seven times to connect all 9 components.

③ End Links

Form the end links of the bracelet:

END LINK, STITCH 1: Use the working thread of the final component to work 3 rows of flat peyote stitch, 3D wide, off of the open 2D of the component's Round 9. Weave through beads to exit out through the last D added (**FIG. 8**).

MAIN COLORWAY

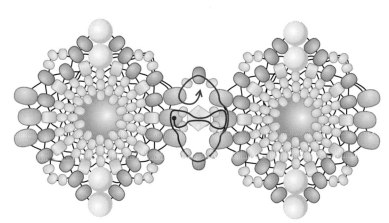

FIG. 7: Adding the link's Stitches 2 and 3

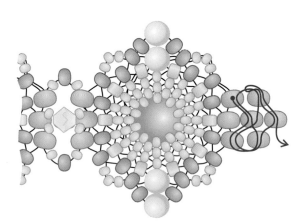

FIG. 8: Forming the end link, Stitch 1

Artist's Tip

- This project works best with tight thread tension. If you tend to bead loosely, waxing your thread can help.

END LINK, STITCH 2: String 1A, 1E, and 1A; pass up through the nearest D of the component's Round 8. String 1A; pass back through the last E added. String 1A; pass through the last D of the previous stitch and back through the nearest D (**FIG. 9, BLUE THREAD**).

END LINK, STITCH 3: String 1A, 1C, and 1A; pass up through the nearest D of the component's Round 9, the following D of Round 8, and the next D of Round 9. String 1A, 1C, and 1A; pass down through the nearest edge D of the end link's Stitch 1 and the next edge D (**FIG. 9, RED THREAD**). Secure the thread and trim.

Start 12" (30.5 cm) of new thread that exits from 1D of the component's Round 9 at the other end of the bracelet. Repeat this entire step for a second end link.

④ Clasp Ring

Use tight tension and tubular peyote stitch to form the clasp ring:

CLASP, ROUNDS 1 AND 2: Use 2' (0.6 m) of thread to string 40A, leaving a 6" (15 cm) tail; pass through all the beads again to form a tight circle, then pass through the first 3A.

CLASP, ROUND 3: String 1A, skip 1A of the previous round, and pass through the next A; repeat nineteen times. Step up for the next and subsequent rounds by passing through the first bead added in the current round.

CLASP, ROUNDS 4 AND 5: Work 2 rounds of 20 stitches with 1B in each stitch.

CLASP, ROUND 6: Work 20 stitches with 1C in each stitch.

CLASP, ROUNDS 7 AND 8: Work 2 rounds of 20 stitches with 1B in each stitch. Weave through beads to exit from Round 1.

ZIP: Fold the beadwork so the clasp's Rounds 1 and 8 interlock like a zipper. Weave through the beads to form a seamless ring. Weave through beads to exit from 1C of the clasp's Round 6.

CONNECTION POINT: String 1B and pass through the next C of the clasp's Round 6; repeat. Pass under the thread between beads and back through the last C exited and the last B added (**FIG. 10, BLUE THREAD, BEADWORK FLATTENED FOR CLARITY**).

LINK: Pass through the D at one end of the bracelet and back through the first C of the connection point (**FIG. 10, RED THREAD**). Repeat the thread path to reinforce. Secure the thread and trim.

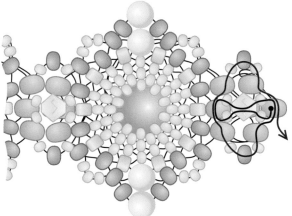

FIG. 9: Adding the end link's Stitches 2 and 3

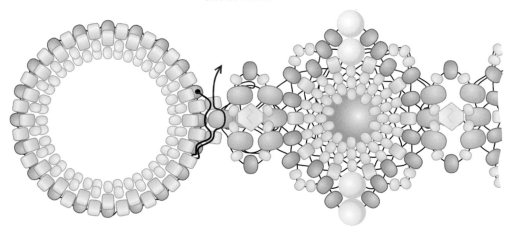

FIG. 10: Connecting the clasp ring

ALTERNATE COLORWAY

⑤ Clasp Bar

Peyote-stitch a toggle bar and connect it to the bracelet:

STRIP: Use 4' (1.2 m) of thread to peyote-stitch a strip 13B wide and 10 rows long.

TUBE: Fold the strip so Rows 1 and 10 interlock like a zipper. Weave through the beads to form a seamless tube. Exit from an edge B, toward the work.

EDGE ROW 1: String 1B and pass through the next B of the same row to "stitch in the ditch"; repeat five times. Pass under the thread between edge beads and back through the last 2B exited (**FIG. 11, GREEN THREAD**).

EDGE ROW 2: Work 2 peyote stitches with 1C in each stitch, 1 stitch with 1A, and 2 stitches with 1C in each stitch. Pass under the thread between edge beads and weave through beads to exit from the third C of this row, toward the center of the work (**FIG. 11, BLUE THREAD**).

CONNECT: String 3A; pass through the D at the free end of the bracelet. String 3A; pass through the second C of Edge Row 2, away from the work (**FIG. 11, RED THREAD**). Repeat the thread path to reinforce, then weave through beads to exit from one end of the tube.

EMBELLISH: String 1F and 1A, then pass back through the F just added and the tube, repeat (**FIG. 12**). Secure the thread and trim.

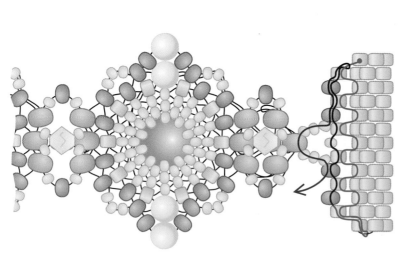

FIG. 11: Adding the clasp bar

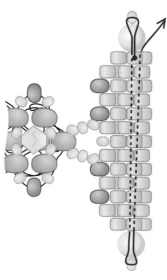

FIG. 12: Embellishing the clasp bar

Double Diamondback

Alice Coelho

technique

Circular peyote stitch

materials

5 g matte blue iris size 15° seed beads (A)

9 g metallic olive size 11° cylinder beads (B)

20 purple velvet 4mm crystal bicones (C)

1 gunmetal 10×31mm 5-strand tube clasp

Smoke 6 lb braided beading thread

tools

Scissors

Size 11 beading needle

finished size

6½" (16.5 cm)

① Square

Use circular peyote stitch to form a square component:

ROUND 1: Use 3' (0.9 cm) of thread to string {1B and 3A} four times, leaving a 6" (15 cm) tail; pass through all the beads again and exit from the first B (**FIG. 1, GREEN THREAD**).

ROUND 2: String 1B, 2A, and 1B, then pass through the next B of Round 1; repeat three times. Step up through the first B added in this round (**FIG. 1, BLUE THREAD**).

ROUND 3: *String 1B, 2A, and 1B; pass through the next B of Round 2. String 1B; pass through the following B of Round 2. Repeat from * three times. Step up through the first B added in this round (**FIG. 1, RED THREAD**).

ROUND 4: **String 1B, 1A, and 1B; pass through the next B of Round 3. Work 2 stitches with 1B in each stitch. Repeat from ** three times. Step up through the first B added in this round (**FIG. 2, GREEN THREAD**).

ROUND 5: ***String 1B, 1A, and 1B; pass through the next B of Round 4. Work 3 stitches with 1B in each stitch. Repeat from *** three times. Pass through the first 1B/1A/1B added; don't trim the thread (**FIG. 2, BLUE THREAD**).

CENTER: Place a needle onto the tail. String 1C; pass through the B on the opposite side of Round 1, back through the C, and through the first B exited (**FIG. 2, RED THREAD**). Repeat the thread path. Secure the thread and trim. Set the square aside.

Repeat this entire step nineteen times for a total of 20 squares.

② Assembly

Join the components:

ROW 1: Use the working thread of 1 square to work 4 stitches with 1B in each stitch down one side of the square (**FIG. 3, BLUE THREAD**).

ZIP: Place the side of the square just worked next to a second square so the beads interlock like a zipper. *NOTE: Take care that the center C of each square lies in the same direction.* Weave the beads together to create a seamless join, passing through the first bead exited on the first square to complete the join (**FIG. 3, RED THREAD**). Secure the working thread of the first square and trim.

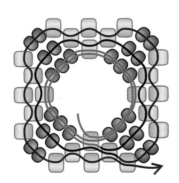

FIG. 1: Forming Rounds 1–3 of the square

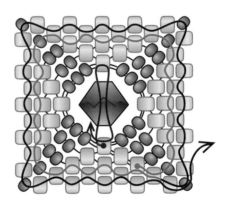

FIG. 2: Adding Rounds 4 and 5 and the center of the square

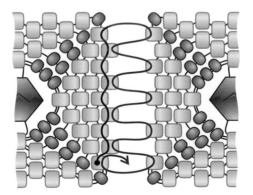

FIG. 3: Stitching the side of the first square and zipping it to another square

Repeat Row 1 and the Zip nine times to join squares end to end, forming a strip of 10 squares, or to the desired length.

ROW 2: As with Row 1, add a row of 4 stitches to one side of 1 new square (**FIG. 4, BLUE THREAD**) and zip it to the top edge of the leftmost square in Row 1 to add the first square in Row 2. Weave through beads to add a row of 4 stitches to the right side of the same square and zip it to the left side of another square to add to Row 2 (**FIG. 4, RED THREAD**). Continue working the second row in the same manner, adding 1 row of 4 stitches between the bottom and right sides of squares and zipping the edges together to attach all the squares. Secure the thread and trim.

Artist's Tips

- When stitching the squares, start with medium tension and gradually increase the tension in each round to keep the squares from warping. Tying knots can also cause the square to warp, so I recommend not using knots.

- You can reinforce any section of the bracelet by just sewing back and forth (or round and round) through the Delicas, since the holes are large.

- The crystals add a bit of glamour but can be left out for a simpler look. Or, try using 4mm pearl rounds instead of crystal bicones.

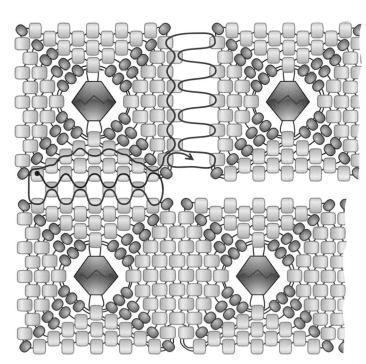

FIG. 4: Adding the first 2 squares of Row 2

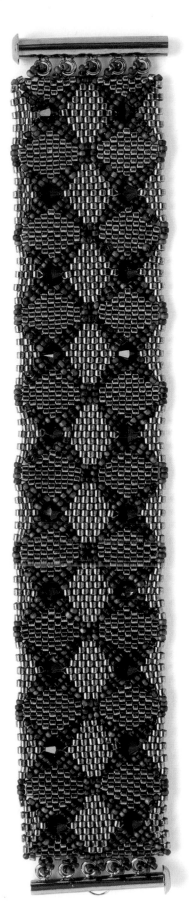

MAIN COLORWAY

INSIDE CORNERS: Start 3' (0.9 m) of new thread that exits from 1A where 4 squares meet. *String 1A and pass through the next A; repeat three times (**FIG. 5, BLUE THREAD**). Pass through the 4A just added again to reinforce (**FIG. 5, RED THREAD**). Weave through beads to exit from an A of the nearest point where the next 4 squares meet; repeat from * to reinforce and tighten the 9 intersecting corners down the center of the bracelet. Secure the thread and trim.

SIDES: Start 3' (0.9 m) of new thread that exits from the lower-right corner A of the first square in Row 1, toward the work. **String 2A; pass through the nearest corner A of the next square and weave through the B along the edge of the bracelet to exit from the next corner A (**FIG. 6**). Repeat from ** along the whole perimeter of the bracelet.

③ Clasp

Weave through beads to exit from the second B on one end of the bracelet, toward the center. ***String 5A and the first loop of one half of the clasp; pass through the last B exited. Repeat the thread path to reinforce, then weave through beads to exit from the 4th B on the end of the bracelet. Repeat from *** to connect to all of the clasp loops, attaching the 4th B to the 2nd loop; the center 2A to the 3rd loop; the 7th B to the 4th loop; and the 9th B to the 5th loop (**FIG. 7**). Secure the thread and trim. Start 12" (30.5 cm) of new thread on the other end of the bracelet and repeat this section to add the other half of the clasp, taking care that it is positioned properly to connect to the first half of the clasp.

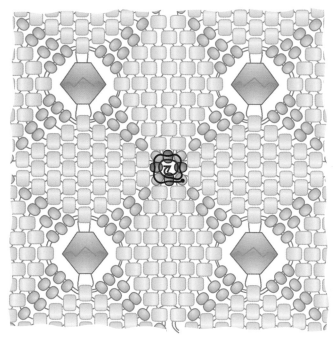

FIG. 5: Stitching the corners together

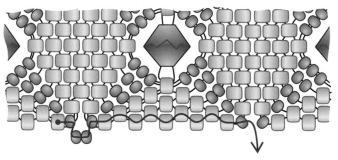

FIG. 6: Filling in the sides of the bracelet

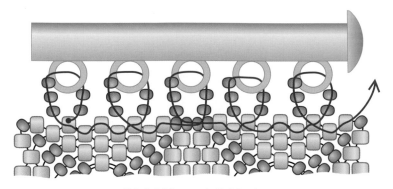

FIG. 7: Adding one half of the clasp

MAIN
COLORWAY

ALTERNATE
COLORWAYS

Bracelet Sizing

Each square is ⅝" (1.6 cm) and the clasp
adds ¼" (6 mm), so you may size your
bracelet accordingly:

20 squares make a 6½" (16.5 cm) bracelet

22 squares make a 7⅛" (18 cm) bracelet

24 squares make a 7¾" (19.5 cm) bracelet

26 squares make an 8⅜" (21 cm) bracelet

Vortices

Kassie Shaw

techniques

Circular peyote stitch

Circular herringbone stitch variation

materials

1 g silver permanent-finish size 11° Japanese seed beads (A)

5 g steel permanent-finish size 11° Japanese seed beads (B)

5 g Bordeaux pastel 5×2.5mm 2-hole SuperDuos (C)

6 g petrol pastel 5×2.5mm 2-hole SuperDuos (D)

2 silver 6mm snap sets

Purple One-G nylon beading thread

tools

Scissors

Size 12 beading needle

finished size

6⅝" (16.5 cm)

❶ Row 1

Use circular peyote stitch and a variation of circular herringbone stitch to work the first row of vortices:

UNIT 1, ROUND 1: Use 2½' (0.8 m) of thread to string 4A, leaving a 4" (10 cm) tail. Pass through the beads again to form a tight circle; use the working and tail threads to tie a square knot and pass through the first A strung (**FIG. 1, BLUE THREAD**).

UNIT 1, ROUND 2: String 1B and pass through the next A of Round 1; repeat three times. Pass through the first B of this round (**FIG. 1, RED THREAD**).

UNIT 1, ROUND 3: String 2B and 1C and pass through the next B of Round 2, then string 2B and 1D and pass through the following B of Round 2; repeat.

Pass through the first 2B of this round (**FIG. 2, BLUE THREAD**).

UNIT 1, ROUND 4: String 2B; pass through the second (outside) hole of the nearest C in Round 3. String 1C; skip the nearest B of the previous round and pass through the next B. String 2B; pass through the nearest D (outside hole) of Round 3. String 1D; skip the nearest B of the previous round and pass through the next B. Repeat from the beginning of this round. Pass through the first 2B of this round (**FIG. 2, RED THREAD**). Weave through beads to exit from 1B of Round 2.

UNIT 1, SNAP: Pass up through one hole in one male half of 1 snap; pass down through the next hole of the same snap and pass through the next B of Round 2 (**FIG. 3, BLUE THREAD**).

Pass up through the last hole exited on the snap, pass down through the next hole of the snap, and pass through the next B of Round 2; repeat twice (**FIG. 3, RED THREAD**). *NOTE: Be sure the snap is faceup. Repeat the thread path of this snap connection twice to reinforce. Secure the threads and trim. Set aside.*

UNIT 2, ROUNDS 1–3: Repeat Unit 1, Rounds 1–3 of Row 1.

UNIT 2, ROUND 4: String 2B; pass through the nearest C (outside hole) of Round 3 in this unit. String 1C; skip the nearest B of the previous round and pass through the next B (**FIG. 4, GREEN THREAD**). String 2B; pass through the nearest D (outside hole) of Round 3 in this unit. String the outside hole of 1D in Unit 1, Round 4; skip the nearest B of the previous round and pass through the

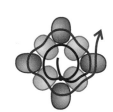

FIG. 1: Working Unit 1, Rounds 1 and 2 of Row 1

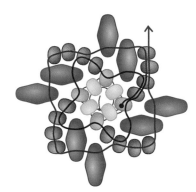

FIG. 2: Stitching Unit 1, Rounds 3 and 4 of Row 1

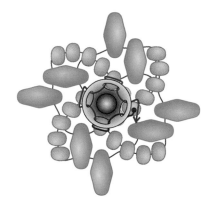

FIG. 3: Adding the snap to Row 1, Unit 1

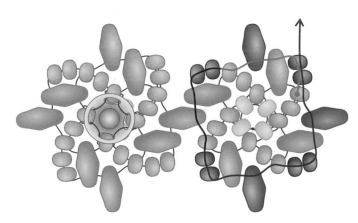

FIG. 4: Forming Unit 2, Round 4 of Row 1

next B (**FIG. 4, BLUE THREAD**). String 2B; pass through the nearest C (outside hole) of Round 3 in this unit. String 1C; skip the nearest B of the previous round and pass through the next B. String 2B; pass through the nearest D (outside hole) of Round 3 in this unit. String 1D; skip the nearest B of the previous round and pass through the next B. Pass through the first 2B of this round (**FIG. 4, RED THREAD**). Weave through beads to exit from 1B of Round 2 in this unit.

UNIT 2, SNAP: Repeat Unit 1, Snap, using the male half of the second snap set.

2 Row 2

Create a second row of vortices that connects to Row 1:

UNIT 1, ROUNDS 1–3: Repeat Unit 1, Rounds 1–3 of Row 1.

UNIT 1, ROUND 4: String 2B; pass through the nearest C (outside hole) of Round 3 in this unit. String the outside hole of the bottom C in Unit 1, Round 4 of the previous row; skip the nearest B of the previous round and pass through the next B (**FIG. 5, BLUE THREAD**). String 2B; pass through the nearest D (outside hole) of Round 3 in this unit. String 1D; skip the nearest B of the previous round and pass through the next B. String 2B; pass through the nearest C (outside hole) of Round 3 in this unit. String 1C; skip the nearest B of the previous round and pass through the next B. String 2B; pass through the nearest D (outside hole) of Round 3 in this unit. String 1D; skip the nearest B of the previous round and pass through the next B. Pass through the first 2B of this round (**FIG. 5, RED THREAD**). Secure the threads and trim. Set aside.

UNIT 2, ROUNDS 1–3: Repeat Unit 1, Rounds 1–3 of Row 1.

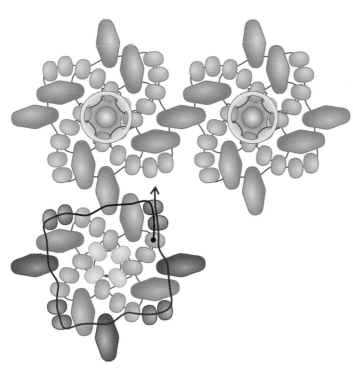

FIG. 5: Working Unit 1, Round 4 of Row 2

MAIN COLORWAY
BACK OF BRACELET

UNIT 2, ROUND 4: String 2B; pass through the nearest C (outside hole) of Round 3 in this unit. String the outside hole of the bottom C in Unit 2, Round 4 of the previous row; skip the nearest B of the previous round and pass through the next B (**FIG. 6, GREEN THREAD**). String 2B; pass through the nearest D (outside hole) of Round 3 in this unit. String the outside hole of the rightmost D in Unit 1, Round 4 of the current row; skip the nearest B of the previous round and pass through the next B (**FIG. 6, BLUE THREAD**). String 2B; pass through the nearest C (outside hole) of Round 3 in this unit. String 1C; skip the nearest B of the previous round and pass through the next B. String 2B; pass through the nearest D (outside hole) of Round 3 in this unit. String 1D; skip the nearest B of the previous round and pass through the next B. Pass through the first 2B of this round (**FIG. 6, RED THREAD**). Secure the threads and trim. Set aside.

3 Rows 3–12

Repeat Step 2 ten times, connecting each new row to the previous row.

4 Row 13

Add the last row of vortices and the second halves of the snap sets:

UNIT 1, ROUNDS 1–4: Repeat Unit 1, Rounds 1–4 of Step 2, but don't trim the working thread. Weave through beads to exit from 1B of Round 2 in this unit, toward the back of the beadwork. Flip the beadwork facedown.

UNIT 1, SNAP: Repeat Unit 1, Snap of Step 1, using one female half of 1 snap set, taking care to add this snap to the opposite side of the beadwork than the male halves added in Step 1, and ensuring that the snap will close properly. Secure the threads and trim. Flip the beadwork faceup.

UNIT 2, ROUNDS 1–4: Repeat Unit 2, Rounds 1–4 of Step 2, but don't trim the working thread. Weave through beads to exit from 1B of Round 2, toward the back of the beadwork. Flip the beadwork facedown.

UNIT 2, SNAP: Repeat Unit 1, Snap of Step 4, attaching the remaining female half of the second snap set as before.

Artist's Tips

- Take care when adding each new unit so that the vortices swirl in the same direction.

- To maintain proper tension when stitching the bracelet, make multiple test units before you begin. If the units are stitched with loose tension, thread will show. If the units are stitched with too tight of tension, the beadwork will cup slightly; if this happens, just make sure that all finished units cup in the same direction.

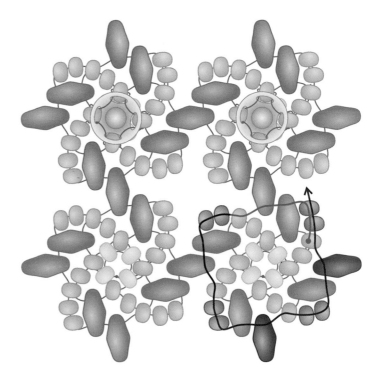

FIG. 6: Stitching Unit 2, Round 4 of Row 2

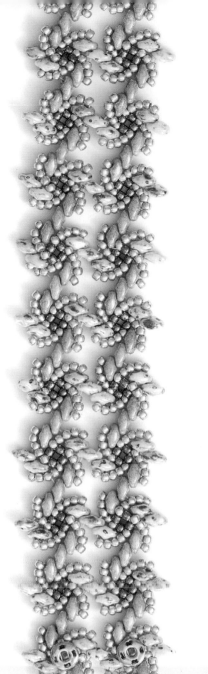

ALTERNATE COLORWAYS
BACKS OF BRACELETS

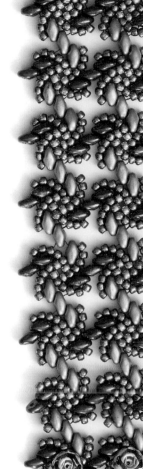

alternate colorway materials

CREAM/TURQUOISE

1 g dusty rose permanent-finish size 11°
  Japanese seed beads (A)

5 g gold permanent-finish size 11°
  Japanese seed beads (B)

5 g chalk green luster 5×2.5mm 2-hole
  SuperDuos (C)

6 g chalk white lazure 5×2.5mm 2-hole
  SuperDuos (D)

2 silver 6mm snap sets

Beige One-G nylon beading thread

PURPLE/BLUE

1 g gold-lined silver-gray size 11°
  Japanese seed beads (A)

5 g higher metallic dragonfly size 11°
  Japanese seed beads (B)

5 g nebula turquoise blue 5×2.5mm
  2-hole SuperDuos (C)

6 g nebula royal blue 5×2.5mm 2-hole
  SuperDuos (D)

2 silver 6mm snap sets

Purple One-G nylon beading thread

GOLD/COPPER

1 g rose gold permanent-finish size 11°
  Japanese seed beads (A)

5 g mauve permanent-finish size 11°
  Japanese seed beads (B)

5 g crystal bronze pale gold 5×2.5mm
  2-hole SuperDuos (C)

6 g coral red iris luster opaque 5×2.5mm
  2-hole SuperDuos (D)

2 silver 6mm snap sets

Brown One-G nylon beading thread

Brick Tracks

Marjorie Schwartz

technique

Flat peyote stitch

materials

0.5 g copper-lined clear size 15° seed beads (A)

2 g metallic bright copper size 11° cylinder beads (B)

41 umber Picasso 6×3mm 2-hole brick beads (C)

1 copper 9mm toggle clasp

Smoke 6 lb braided beading thread

tools

Scissors

Size 11 beading needle

finished size

7¾" (19.5 cm)

① Base

Use 3' (0.9 m) of thread to string {1C and 1B} forty times, leaving a 6" (15 cm) tail. String 1C and 2B; pass through the second hole in the last C strung. String 1B and pass through the second hole in the next C; repeat thirty-nine times. String 2B; tie a square knot with the working and tail threads. Pass through the first hole of the first C in this step and the following B (**FIG. 1**).

② Embellishment

Use flat peyote stitch to form picotlike edging:

ROUND 1: String 2B and pass through the next B on the edge of the base; repeat thirty-eight times for a total of 78B (**FIG. 2, GREEN THREAD**). String 2B and 2A; pass through the 2B on the nearest end of the base. String 2A and 2B; pass through the nearest B on the other edge of the bracelet (**FIG. 2, BLUE THREAD**). Repeat from the beginning of this round. Step up through the first 1B of this round (**FIG. 2, RED THREAD**).

ROUND 2: String 1A; pass through the next 1B of the previous round, the following 1B of the base, and the following 1B of the previous round. Repeat from the beginning of this round thirty-nine times for a total of 40A. Weave through beads to exit through the first 1B on the other edge of the bracelet. String 1A and pass through the next 1B of the previous round, the following 1B of the base, and the following 1B of the previous round; repeat forty times to finish this edge of the bracelet. Weave through beads to exit the second-to-last B added in Round 1. String 1A; pass through the next 1B of Round 1, the following 1B of the base, and the following 1B of Round 1 (**FIG. 3**). Secure the thread and trim.

FIG. 1: Stringing the base of the bracelet

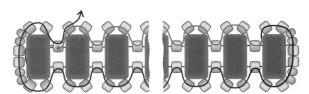

FIG. 2: Working Round 1 of the embellishment

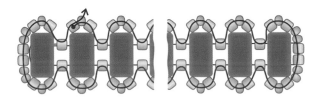

FIG. 3: Stitching Round 2 of the embellishment

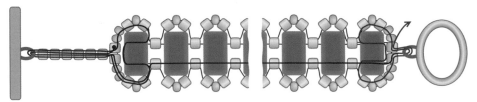

FIG. 4: Adding the clasp

3 Clasp

Start 12" (30.5 cm) of new thread that exits from 1B on one end of the bracelet, toward the next B. String 6B and the bar half of the clasp; pass back through the 6B just added and through the next B on the end of the bracelet. Weave through beads to exit from the first B exited at the beginning of this step and repeat the thread path to reinforce. Weave through beads to exit 1B on the other end of the bracelet (**FIG. 4, BLUE THREAD**). String the ring half of the clasp; pass through the following B on the end of the bracelet. Weave through beads to repeat the thread path (**FIG. 4, RED THREAD**). Secure the thread and trim.

Artist's Tips

- The clasp adds ¾" (2 cm) to the finished length of the embellished base, so select the clasp first and measure for length. Add this to the length of the base for the correct finished length.

- Start a new thread to add the clasp rather than using the tail or working thread. This way, clasps can be changed without damaging the bracelet threads. If you change the clasp, be extra careful not to cut the thread between the 2B at the end of the bracelet.

MAIN COLORWAY

ALTERNATE COLORWAYS

Sultan's Treasure

Maria Teresa Moran

techniques

Fringe

Circular peyote stitch

Picot

materials

5 g silver-lined brown size 15° seed beads (A)

5 g bronze size 11° seed beads (B)

10 g transparent cherry-red 6mm twisted bugle beads (C)

18 amethyst 4mm crystal bicones (D)

52 light rose 4mm crystal bicones (E)

1 copper 14×18mm fancy toggle clasp

Smoke 6 lb braided beading thread

tools

Scissors

Size 12 beading needle

finished size

7¼" (18.5 cm)

MAIN COLORWAY

① Row 1

Use seed beads, bugle beads, and crystals to form the first row of the bracelet band:

UNIT 1, ROUND 1: Use 3' (0.9 m) of thread to string {1B and 1C} four times, leaving a 15" (38 cm) tail. Use the tail and working threads to tie a square knot to form a tight circle of beads. Pass through the first B/C (**FIG. 1, GREEN THREAD**).

UNIT 1, ROUND 2: String 2B and pass through the next C of Round 1; repeat three times. Step up through the first B added in this round (**FIG. 1, BLUE THREAD**).

UNIT 1, ROUND 3: String 1B and pass through the next B of the previous round, then string 1C and pass through the following B; repeat. String 1B; pass through the next B of the previous round, then string 1C and pass back through the first B of the connector, the corner B of the previous unit, and the third B of the connector. String 1C and pass through the next B. Weave through beads to exit from the bottom center B in Round 1 of this unit (**FIG. 4, PURPLE THREAD**).

UNIT 1, ROUND 4: String 4A and pass through the next B of Round 1; repeat three times (**FIG. 2, BLUE THREAD**).

UNIT 1, CENTER FRINGE: String 1B, 1D, and 1B; pass through the B of Round 1 opposite the one just exited. Pass back through the 1B/1D/1B and through the original B exited. Weave through beads to exit from the nearest corner B of Round 3 (**FIG. 2, PURPLE THREAD**).

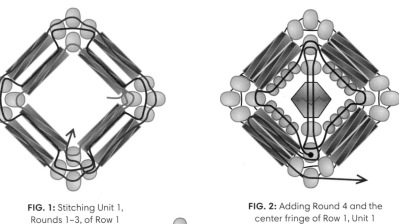

FIG. 1: Stitching Unit 1, Rounds 1–3, of Row 1

FIG. 2: Adding Round 4 and the center fringe of Row 1, Unit 1

FIG. 3: Forming the bottom fringe and connector of Row 1, Unit 1

UNIT 1, BOTTOM FRINGE: String 2B, 1E, and 3A; pass back through the E just added to form a picot. String 2B; pass through the last corner B exited in Round 3. Weave through beads to exit from the next corner B of Round 3 (**FIG. 3, BLUE THREAD**).

UNIT 1, CONNECTOR: String 3B; pass through the last corner B exited in Round 3 and the first 2B just added (**FIG. 3, RED THREAD**).

UNIT 2, ROUND 1: String {1C and 1B} three times. String 1C and pass through the second B added in the connector and the first C added in this round (**FIG. 4, GREEN THREAD**).

UNIT 2, ROUND 2: String 2B and pass through the next C of the previous round; repeat twice. Pass back through the first and third B added in the connector, the next C, and the first B added in this round (**FIG. 4, BLUE THREAD**).

UNIT 2, ROUND 3: String 1B and pass through the next B of the previous round, then string 1C and pass through the

following B; repeat. String 1B; pass through the next B of the previous round, then string 1C and pass back through the first B of the connector. Weave through beads to exit from the bottom center B in Round 1 of this unit (**FIG. 4, PURPLE THREAD**).

UNIT 2, ROUND 4, CENTER AND BOTTOM FRINGE, AND CONNECTOR: Repeat Round 4, the center and bottom fringe, and the connector of Unit 1.

UNITS 3–9: Repeat Unit 2 seven times or to the desired length minus 1" (2.5 cm) for the clasp, but don't add the connector to Unit 9. Weave through beads to exit from the corner B in Round 4 of the final unit that's opposite the fringe, toward the start of the band.

② Row 2

Stitch a second row of square units:

UNIT 1, BOTTOM CONNECTOR: String 3B and pass through the last B exited in Round 4 of the previous Row 1 unit and the first 2B just added (**FIG. 5, ORANGE THREAD**).

UNIT 1, ROUND 1: String {1C and 1B} three times. String 1C and pass through the second B added in the connector and the first C added in this round (**FIG. 5, GREEN THREAD**).

UNIT 1, ROUND 2: String 2B and pass through the next C of Round 1; repeat twice. Pass back through the first and third B added in the connector. Weave through beads to exit from the first B added in this round (**FIG. 5, BLUE THREAD**).

UNIT 1, ROUND 3: String 1B and pass through the next B of Round 2, then string 1C and pass through the next B of Round 2; repeat. String 1B; pass through the next B of Round 2. String 1C; pass back through the first B of the connector, through the corner B in Round 4 of the Row 1 unit, and back through the third B of the connector. String 1C; pass through the next B of Round 2. Weave through beads to exit from the B of Round 1 opposite the connector added in this unit (**FIG. 5, PURPLE THREAD**).

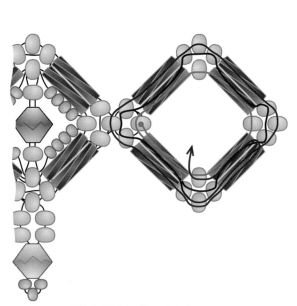

FIG. 4: Stitching Rounds 1–3 of Row 1, Unit 2

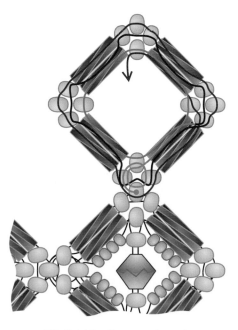

FIG. 5: Adding the connector and Rounds 1–3 of Row 2, Unit 1

UNIT 1, ROUND 4, CENTER, TOP FRINGE, AND SIDE CONNECTOR: Repeat Round 4 (**FIG. 6, GREEN THREAD**), the center and bottom fringe (**FIG. 6, BLUE THREAD**), and the connector of Row 1, Unit 1, but this time add the bottom fringe to the top of Row 2 and stitch the side connector so it sits on the inside corner of the unit. Weave through beads to exit from the top corner B of the next unit in Row 1 (**FIG. 6, PURPLE THREAD**).

UNITS 2–9: Repeat Unit 1 eight times, incorporating the bottom and side connectors to the rounds as before; don't add the side connector to Unit 9. Secure the thread and trim.

③ Embellishment

Start 4' (1.2 m) of new thread that exits up through the shared connector B between Units 1 and 2 of Row 1, leaving an 8" (20.5 cm) tail. *String 2A, 1E, 1B, 1E, and 2A; pass through the shared connector B between Units 8 and 9 of Row 2. Weave through beads to exit the shared connector B between Unit 1 of Row 1 and Unit 9 of Row 2 (**FIG. 7, BLUE THREAD**). String 2A and 1E, pass through the last B added in this step, then string 1E and 2A; pass through the shared connector B between Unit 2 of Row 1 and Unit 8 of Row 2. Repeat the thread path to reinforce. Weave through beads to exit up through the next shared connector B of Row 1 (**FIG. 7, PURPLE THREAD**). Repeat from * to embellish between each set of Row 1 and Row 2 units.

④ Clasp

Weave through beads to exit up through a corner B in Round 3 of Row 1, Unit 9. String 5B, 1E, 3B, one half of the clasp, and 3B; pass back through the last E strung. String 5B and pass up through the corner B in Round 3 of Row 2, Unit 1 (**FIG. 8**). Repeat the thread path to reinforce. Secure the working thread and trim. Place a needle on the tail thread and repeat this step to add the other half of the clasp to the other end of the bracelet.

FIG. 6: Stitching Round 4, the center, top fringe, and side connector of Row 2, Unit 1

FIG. 7: Embellishing the band

Artist's Tip

- It's always a good idea to use good-quality beads and findings. Not only do they fit better, but they look wonderful.

Fig. 8: Adding the clasp

ALTERNATE COLORWAY

Moroccan Sunset

Shae Wilhite

technique

Peyote stitch variation

materials

0.5 g metallic bronze size 11° seed beads (A)

2 g African sunset gold luster size 8° seed beads (B)

0.5 g metallic bronze size 8° seed beads (C)

72 matte gold 8×5mm 2-hole DiamonDuos (D)

70 turquoise Picasso 8×5mm 2-hole DiamonDuos (E)

72 pumpkin pie 8×5mm 2-hole DiamonDuos (F)

35 coral pecan lumi 8×5mm 2-hole DiamonDuos (G)

1 antiqued brass 35×25mm 7-strand decorative box clasp

Smoke 6 lb FireLine braided beading thread

tools

Scissors

Size 10 or 11 beading needle

finished size

8¼" (21 cm)

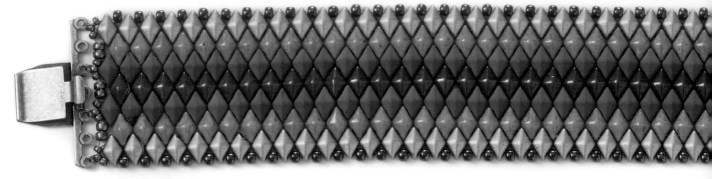

MAIN COLORWAY

① Band

Use a variation of peyote stitch to form the bracelet band:

ROWS 1 AND 2: *NOTE: Take care to string each DiamonDuo so that the faceted side is faceup; the smooth side of the bead is the back.* Add a stop bead to 12' (3.7 m) of thread, leaving a 4" (10 cm) tail. String {1D and 1B} thirty-five times (**FIG. 1, PURPLE THREAD**). String 1D and 3A; pass through the unused (second) hole of the last D added (**FIG. 1, GREEN THREAD**).

ROW 3: String 1E and pass through the nearest DiamonDuo (second hole) of the previous row; repeat thirty-four times (**FIG. 1, BLUE THREAD**). String 2C and 1F; pass through the last E (second hole) added (**FIG. 1, RED THREAD**).

ROW 4: Work 34 peyote stitches using F and passing through the second holes of the DiamonDuos in the previous row (**FIG. 2, BLUE THREAD**). String 1F and 3A; pass through the last F (second hole) added (**FIG. 2, RED THREAD**).

ROW 5: Repeat Row 3, using G for E.

ROW 6: Repeat Row 4.

ROW 7: Repeat Row 3, using D for F.

ROW 8: Repeat Row 4, using D for F.

ROW 9: Work 35 peyote stitches using B and passing through the second holes of the D in the previous row (**FIG. 3, PURPLE THREAD**).

② Ends

String 3A and pass back through the nearest 2C of the base; repeat twice. String 3A; pass through the nearest D (first hole) of the band (**FIG. 3, GREEN THREAD**). Weave through beads to exit from the last D (first hole) of the current row at the other end of the band and the nearest 3A (**FIG. 3, BLUE THREAD**). String 2C and pass through the next 3A of the band; repeat twice. Weave through beads to exit from the first 2A of this step (**FIG. 3, RED THREAD**).

③ Clasp

NOTE: Take care to attach each half of the clasp so that the front faces the same direction as the front of the band. String the end loop of one half of the clasp, then pass through the last A exited and weave through beads as shown in **FIG. 4** to exit from the first 2A of the next 3A set at this end of the band (**FIG. 4, GREEN THREAD**); repeat twice, stringing every other loop of the clasp (**FIG. 4, BLUE THREAD**). String the last loop of the same half of the clasp, then pass through the last A exited and weave through beads as shown in **FIG. 4** to exit from the first 2A of the nearest 3A set at the other end of the band (**FIG. 4, RED THREAD**).

Repeat this entire step to attach the second half of the clasp to the other end of the band. Repeat the thread path of this entire step to reinforce. Secure the working thread and trim. Remove the stop bead; secure the tail thread and trim.

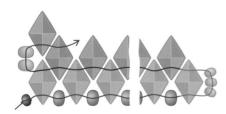

FIG. 1: Working Rows 1–3

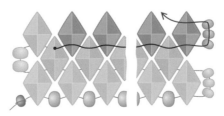

FIG. 2: Forming Row 4

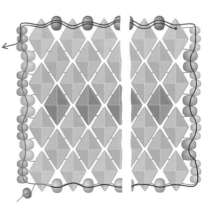

FIG. 3: Adding Row 9 and stitching the ends

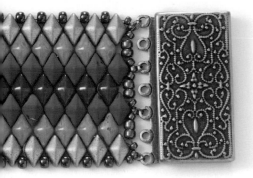

Artist's Tips

- You can adjust the length of the bracelet by increasing or decreasing the number of DiamonDuos strung in Row 1, but make sure you start with an even number of DiamonDuos in the first row. Each DiamonDuo/size 8° seed bead/ DiamonDuo set equals about ³⁄₁₆" (0.5 cm).

- To add a touch of sparkle, substitute 2mm crystal or fire-polished rounds for the size 8° seed beads in Rows 1 and 9.

ALTERNATE COLORWAY

alternate colorway materials

0.5 g African sunset gold luster size 11° seed beads (A)

3 g African sunset gold luster size 8° seed beads (B; use for Material C in main colorway.)

There is no C in this colorway.

68 purple iris 8×5mm 2-hole DiamonDuos (D)

66 matte copper 8×5mm 2-hole DiamonDuos (E)

68 moss green 8×5mm 2-hole DiamonDuos (F)

33 Bordeaux pastel 8×5mm 2-hole DiamonDuos (G)

1 antiqued copper 35×25mm 7-strand decorative box clasp

Smoke 6 lb FireLine braided beading thread

finished size

7 ⅞" (20.5 cm)

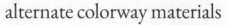

FIG. 4: Attaching the clasp

Saturn Connections

Carole Ohl

techniques

Circular herringbone stitch

Ladder stitch

materials

0.5 g light smoky pewter galvanized size 15° seed beads (A)

5 g light smoky pewter galvanized size 11° seed beads (B)

2 g matte metallic blue slate AB size 11° cylinder beads (C)

9 polychrome orchid aqua 6mm pressed-glass rounds (D)

1 silver 16×10mm 2-strand tube clasp

Smoke 4 lb FireLine braided beading thread

tools

Scissors

Size 11 or 12 beading needle

finished size

7" (18 cm)

① Components

Use circular herringbone stitch and ladder stitch to make the components:

ROUND 1: Use 2' (0.6 m) of thread to string 16B, leaving a 4" (10 cm) tail. Pass through the beads twice to form a circle and exit through the first B strung (**FIG. 1, GREEN THREAD**).

CENTER: String 1D; pass back through the eighth through first beads strung in Round 1 (**FIG. 1, BLUE THREAD**). Pass through the D; pass through the ninth through sixteenth beads strung in Round 1. Pass through the first 2B of Round 1 (**FIG. 1, RED THREAD**).

ROUND 2: String 2B and pass through the next 4B of Round 1 to form a herringbone stitch; repeat three times. *NOTE: For this and subsequent rounds, step up through the first bead added in the current round* (**FIG. 2, BLUE THREAD**).

ROUND 3: String 2B and pass down through the next B of the previous round to form a herringbone stitch, then string 4C and pass up through the following B of the previous round; repeat three times (**FIG. 2, RED THREAD**).

ROUND 4: String 2B and pass down through the next B of the previous round to form a herringbone stitch, then string 6C and pass up through the following B of the previous round; repeat three times (**FIG. 3, GREEN THREAD**).

ROUND 5: String 2B and pass down through the next B of the previous round to form a herringbone stitch, then weave through beads to pass up through the following B of the previous round; repeat three times. Weave through beads to exit from the nearest 5C of Round 4 (**FIG. 3, BLUE THREAD**).

LINK: String 4B; pass through the last 4C exited and the 4B just added (**FIG. 3, RED THREAD**). Pass through the last 4C exited and the 4B just added to reinforce. Secure the threads and trim. Set aside.

Repeat this entire step eight times for a total of 9 components.

② Assembly

Use ladder stitch to connect the components:

TOP CONNECTION: Add a stop bead to 6' (1.8 cm) of new thread, leaving a 16" (40.5 cm) tail. With the component's link to the right, pass up through the top 5C at the left side of 1 component. *NOTE: The center 6mm round will be raised on one side of each component, creating the front; when connecting the components, take care that each component is faceup. Weave through*

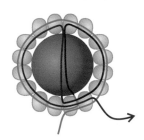

FIG. 1: Stitching Round 1 and adding the center of a component

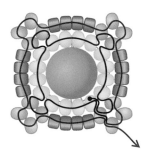

FIG. 2: Working Rounds 2 and 3 of a component

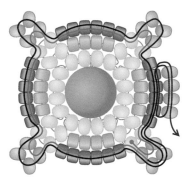

FIG. 3: Finishing Rounds 4 and 5 and the link of a component

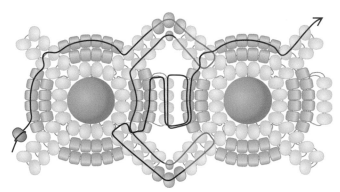

FIG. 4: Connecting the components

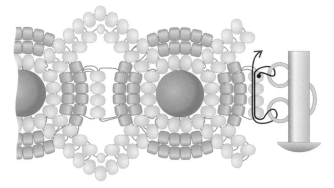

FIG. 5: Attaching the clasp

beads to exit up through the top B of Round 5 at the herringbone-stitched corner above the link (**FIG. 4, PINK THREAD**). *Align 1 new component next to the previous component, with the new component's link to the right. String 3B; pass down through the mirror B of the new component and weave through beads to exit up through the B of the new component next to the last B exited (**FIG. 4, ORANGE THREAD**). String 1A; pass down through the mirror B of the first component and weave through beads to exit down through the top B at the end of the herringbone-stitched corner below the first component's link (**FIG. 4, PURPLE THREAD**).

BOTTOM CONNECTION: String 1A; pass up through the mirror B of the new component and weave through beads to exit down through the B of the new component next to the last B exited (**FIG. 4, GREEN THREAD**). String 3B; pass up through the mirror B of the first component and weave through beads to exit down through the 4B of the first component's link (**FIG. 4, BLUE THREAD**).

CENTER CONNECTION: Pass up through the center 4C of the nearest edge in the new component. Pass through the last

4B exited on the previous component and the last 4C exited on the new component. Weave through beads to exit up through the top B of Round 5 at the herringbone-stitched corner above the new component's link (**FIG. 4, RED THREAD**).

Repeat from * seven times to connect the remaining components, but after the last repeat, weave through beads of the last component added to exit up through the 4B of its link.

3 Clasp 1

String one loop of one half of the clasp and pass back through the last 4B exited (**FIG. 5, BLUE THREAD**); repeat, stringing the second loop of the same half of the clasp (**FIG. 5, RED THREAD**). Repeat the thread path of this step twice. Secure and trim the working thread.

4 Clasp 2

Remove the stop bead. Add a needle to the tail thread. String 4B and pass through the last 4C exited and the 4B just added; repeat the thread path to reinforce. Repeat Step 3, using the second half of the clasp and taking care that the halves are positioned to close properly.

Artist's Tips

- Use only galvanized round seed beads. Different finishes can affect the size of seed beads, which might result in an uneven look.

- Knots aren't required in this project. Numerous thread reinforcements keep the beads in place and provide the structure needed for the turnarounds.

- Using tight tension is recommended.

Caliente

Michelle Gowland

techniques

Circular peyote stitch

Circular netting

Picot

materials

1.5 g metallic green iris size 15° seed beads (A)

0.5 g matte metallic copper iris size 15° seed beads (B)

2 g dark bronze size 15° seed beads (C)

8 total dark bronze size 11° seed beads (D)

0.5 g light travertine Picasso size 8° seed beads (E)

3.5 g lava red 3.8×11mm O beads (F)

1 g matte peridot vitrail 3.8×1mm O beads (G)

5 g metallic gold 5mm 2-hole Es-o beads (H)

3 g lemon dark travertine 5×2.5 mm 2-hole SuperDuos (J)

3 g opaque red luster 5×2.5mm 2-hole SuperDuos (K)

48 turquoise 5 mm 2-hole RounDuos (L)

9 metallic copper 8 mm 2-hole Tipp beads (M)

48 topaz 2.5×1.5 mm crystal rondelles (N)

1 antiqued copper 8×14 mm round magnetic clasp

Crystal 4 lb FireLine braided beading thread

Beeswax

tools

Scissors

Size 10 beading needle

finished size

8¹⁄₁₆" (21 cm) (with ¹¹⁄₁₆" [3 cm] medallions)

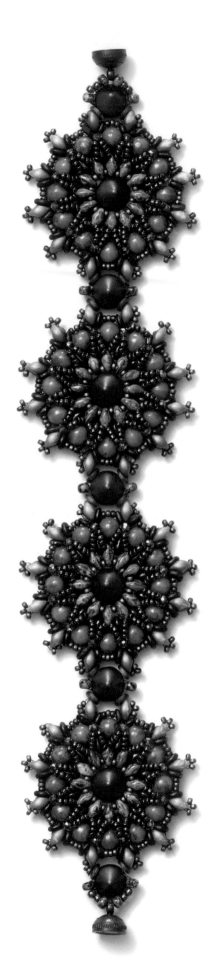

① Medallions

Use a variation of circular peyote stitch, circular netting, and picots to form the medallions:

CENTER: Position 1M faceup on your work surface with the holes oriented horizontally. Working clockwise, use 4' of waxed thread to string 1M (top then bottom holes), leaving a 4" (10 cm) tail. Use the working and tail threads to tie a knot. Pass through the top hole of the M.

ROUND 1: String {1A and 1J} four times. String 1A; pass through the M (top then bottom holes) (**FIG. 1, GREEN THREAD**). String {1A and 1J} four times. String 1A; pass through the M (bottom then top holes). Pass through the first set of beads in this round (same holes of the J), exiting from the fifth A (**FIG. 1, BLUE THREAD**). String 1J, 1A, and 1J and pass through the next set of beads in this round (same holes of the J); repeat, then repeat the thread path to reinforce. Pass through the first (inside) then second (outside) holes of the next J (**FIG. 1, RED THREAD**). *NOTE: You'll now begin working in the opposite direction.*

ROUND 2: String 1K and pass through the next J (outside hole) of the previous round; repeat eleven times, then repeat the thread path to reinforce. Pass through the first (inside) then second (outside) holes of the first K in this round (**FIG. 2, GREEN THREAD**). *NOTE: You'll now begin working in the opposite direction.*

ROUND 3: *NOTE: Take care to string each L so the front faces the same direction as the front of the M.* String 1L and pass through the next K (outside hole) of the previous round; repeat eleven times, then repeat the thread path to reinforce. Form a "tension knot" by tying an overhand knot on the nearest thread between beads in this round, taking care that the beads are snug. Repeat the thread path of this round and pass through the first (inside) then second (outside) holes of the first L in this round (**FIG. 2, BLUE THREAD**). *NOTE: You'll now begin working in the opposite direction.*

FIG. 1: Stitching Medallion, Round 1

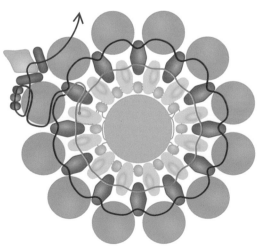

FIG. 2: Working Medallion, Rounds 2–4

ROUND 4: String 1B, 1A, and 1B and pass through the last L (outside hole) exited, then string 1F, 1H, and 1F and pass through the next L (outside hole) of the previous round (**FIG. 2, RED THREAD**); repeat eleven times.

ROUND 5: String 1N and 4C; pass through the next J (outside hole) of Round 1. String 4C and 1N; skip the next L of Round 3 and pass through the following L (outside hole) (**FIG. 3, GREEN THREAD**). Repeat from the beginning of this round five times. Pass through the first N of this round (**FIG. 3, BLUE THREAD**). *NOTE: You'll now begin working in the opposite direction.* String 4C and pass through the next J (outside hole) of Round 1, then string 4C and pass back through the nearest N, the next L (outside hole), and the following N (**FIG. 3, RED THREAD**); repeat five times. Weave through beads to exit from the nearest H (inside then outside holes) of Round 4.

ROUND 6: String 3A and pass through the last H (outside then inside holes) exited, then weave through beads to exit from the next H (inside then outside holes) (**FIG. 4, GREEN THREAD**); repeat three times but on the third repeat don't pass through the outside hole of the next H (**FIG. 4, BLUE THREAD**). Weave through beads to exit from the second H (inside then outside holes) from the last H exited (**FIG. 4, RED THREAD**). Repeat from the beginning of this round, exiting from the inside hole of the last unembellished H. Secure and trim the tail thread but don't trim the working thread. Set aside.

Repeat this entire step three times for a total of 4 medallions.

Artist's Tips

- When connecting the medallions, it might help to turn them facedown and work from the back.

- Use new threads to attach the halves of the clasps rather than using the working threads of the end medallions. If you need to make adjustments to the clasp connection later, you can just cut the clasp thread and rework only that portion without causing damage to the rest of the bracelet.

- Don't keep more than one magnetic clasp open on your work surface at a time; you might accidentally add two opposing halves to your work.

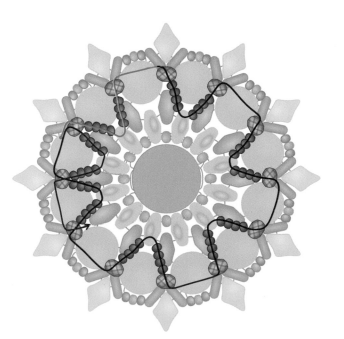

FIG. 3: Forming Medallion, Round 5

FIG. 4: Adding Medallion, Round 6

② Assembly

Connect the medallions:

PASS 1: *NOTE: Take care to connect the components faceup and to string the new M faceup.* Use the working thread of 1 medallion to string 3A; pass through the outside hole of the last H exited. String 1G, 1M, and 1G; pass through the nearest unembellished H (outside hole) of the last component exited. String 3A; pass through the inside hole of the H and the next 1F, 1L (outside hole), 1F, 1H (inside hole), 3A, 1H (outside hole), 1G, and 1M (first hole) (**FIG. 5, GREEN THREAD**).

PASS 2: String 1E; pass through the second hole of the M. String 1E; pass through the first hole of the M, the first E just added, and the second hole of the M (**FIG. 5, BLUE THREAD**).

PASS 3: String 1G; pass up through the outside hole of the top-left unembellished H of 1 new medallion. String 3A; pass through the inside hole of the last H exited and the next 1F, 1L (outside hole), 1F, and 1H (inside hole). String 3A; pass through the outside hole of the H. String 1G; pass through the last M (second hole) exited (**FIG. 5, RED THREAD**). Weave through beads and repeat the thread path of this connection to reinforce. Secure and trim the working thread.

Repeat this entire step twice, using the working thread of the last component added to form the next connection opposite the previous connection. Secure and trim the working thread of the last component added.

③ Clasp

Attach the clasp to the ends of the bracelet:

PASSES 1 AND 2: Start 2' (0.6 m) of new thread that exits from the inside hole of 1 unembellished H at the outside edge of 1 end component, away from the beadwork. Repeat Step 2, Passes 1 and 2.

PASS 3: String 1D, 1E, one half of the clasp, 1E, and 1D; pass through the M (second hole), the nearest E of Pass 2 in the clasp, the M (first hole), and the next E of Pass 2 in the clasp (**FIG. 6, BLUE THREAD**).

PASS 4: String 1D; pass through the next 1D/1E/clasp/1E/1D. String 1D; pass through the next E (**FIG. 6, RED THREAD**). Weave through beads and repeat the thread path of this step to reinforce. Secure and trim the threads.

Repeat this entire step at the other end of the bracelet, using the second half of the clasp.

FIG. 5: Connecting the medallions

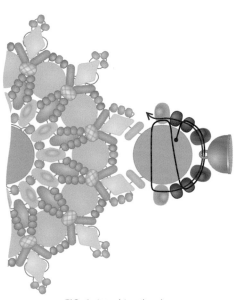

FIG. 6: Attaching the clasp

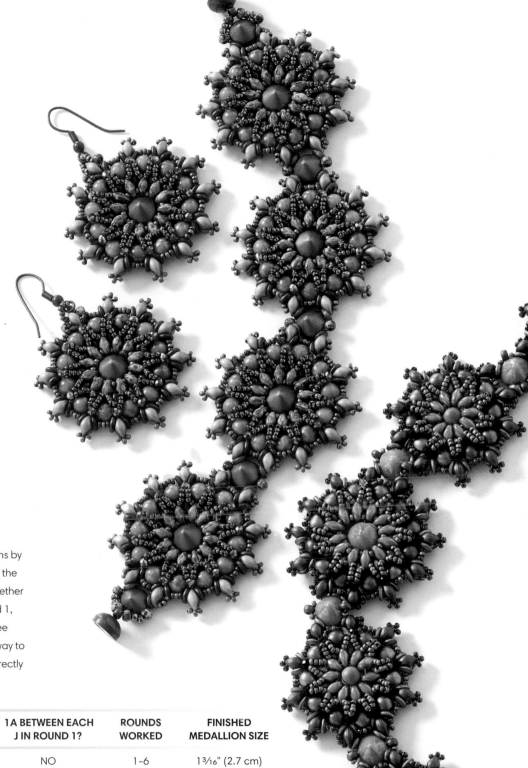

variation

You can alter the size of the medallions by adjusting the size of the center bead, the number of SuperDuos in Round 1, whether you use size 15º seed beads in Round 1, and the number of rounds worked. See the chart below to determine which way to make your medallions in order to correctly size your bracelet before you start.

CENTER BEAD SIZE	NUMBER OF J IN ROUND 1	1A BETWEEN EACH J IN ROUND 1?	ROUNDS WORKED	FINISHED MEDALLION SIZE
5 mm	10	NO	1-6	1³⁄₁₆" (2.7 cm)
8 mm	10	NO	1-6	1½" (3.8 cm)
8 mm	10	YES	1-6	1⅝" (4 cm)
8 mm	10	YES	1-6	1¹¹⁄₁₆" (4.3 cm)

Peyote Points

Julie Glasser

technique

Odd-count flat peyote stitch

Brick stitch

materials

1 g size 11° cylinder beads in shell pink luster (A)

1 g size 11° galvanized satin-finish muscat (B)

1 g size 11° galvanized satin-finish berry (C)

1 g size 11° galvanized dusty mauve (D)

1 g size 11° galvanized pale lavender (E)

1 g size 11° rose-lined crystal (F)

1 g size 11° galvanized cranberry (G)

1 g size 11° galvanized satin-finish light smoky amethyst (H)

1 g size 11° galvanized earth gold iris (I)

1 g size 11° sparkling bright pink–lined clear (J)

1 g size 11° light metallic lavender (K)

1 clear 8mm sew-on snap set

Pink size D nylon beading thread

Thread conditioner

tools

Scissors

Size 10 beading needles

finished size

7" (18 cm)

1 Base

Work odd-count flat peyote stitch to form the body of the bracelet:

ROWS 1 AND 2: Add a stop bead to one end of 6' (1.8 m) of conditioned thread, leaving a 6" (15 cm) tail. String 133 beads in this color order: 6A, 2B, 1C, 2B, 13D, 1B, 11D, 2B, 8E, 2B, 9D, 2B, 5F, 2B, 8G, 2B, 1F, 2B, 4E, 2B, 1H, 2B, 9G, 1B, 6C, 1B, 6I, 2B, 3F, 2B, and 15J.

ROW 3: String 1J, skip 1J of the previous row, and pass back through the next J. Work 66 odd-count peyote stitches with 1 bead in each stitch for a total of 67 beads in this row. Follow the chart for color placement in this and subsequent rows (**FIG. 1**). Remove the stop bead and use the working and tail threads to tie a secure knot. Step up for the next row by passing back through the last bead added.

ROW 4: Work 7 stitches with 1 bead in each stitch, then work 1 stitch with 2 beads; repeat twice. Work 8 stitches with 1 bead in each stitch, then work 1 stitch with 2 beads; repeat. Work 7 stitches with 1 bead in each stitch, then work 1 stitch with 2 beads; repeat. Work 8 stitches with 1 bead in each stitch for a total of 73 beads in this row (**FIG. 2, PURPLE THREAD**).

ROW 5: Work 74 stitches with 1 bead in each stitch, splitting the 2-bead sets of the previous row (**FIG. 2, ORANGE THREAD**). At the end of this and each subsequent odd-numbered row, form a turnaround by passing under the thread between edge beads of the previous 2 rows and stepping up for the next row by passing back through the last bead added, unless otherwise noted.

ROW 6: Work 73 stitches with 1 bead in each stitch (**FIG. 2, GREEN THREAD**).

ROW 7: Work 9 stitches with 1 bead in each stitch, then pass back through the next bead of Row 6 to form a decrease. Work 8 stitches with 1 bead in each stitch, then pass back through the next bead of Row 6 to form a decrease; repeat. Work 9 stitches with 1 bead in each stitch, then form a decrease; repeat. Work 8 stitches with 1 bead in each stitch, then form a decrease; repeat. Work 8 stitches with 1 bead in each stitch for a total of 67 beads in this row (**FIG. 2, BLUE THREAD**).

ROW 8: Work 66 stitches with 1 bead in each stitch. *NOTE: You will add 1 bead over the decreases of the previous row* (**FIG. 2, RED THREAD**).

ROWS 9–11: Work 3 rows (67 stitches, 66 stitches, 67 stitches).

ROWS 12–14: Repeat Rows 4–6.

MAIN COLORWAY

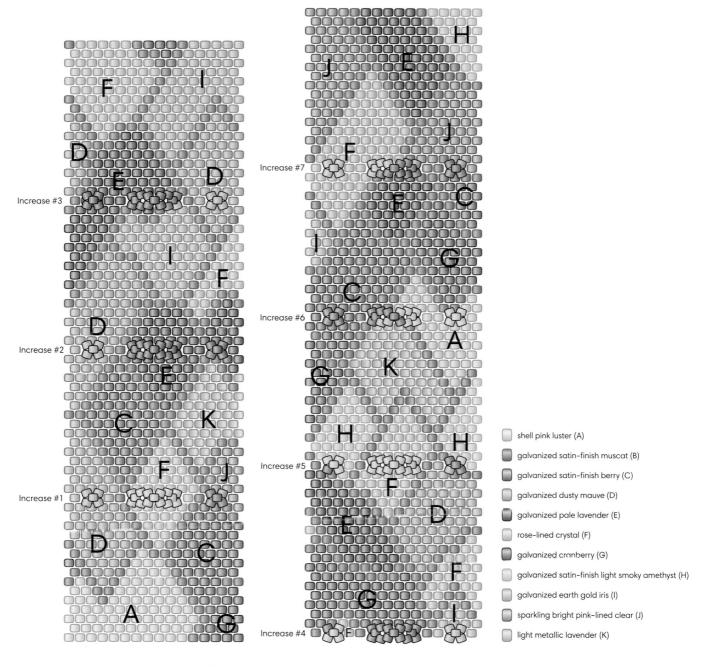

FIG. 1: Base color chart (Rotate 90°)

shell pink luster (A)

galvanized satin-finish muscat (B)

galvanized satin-finish berry (C)

galvanized dusty mauve (D)

galvanized pale lavender (E)

rose-lined crystal (F)

galvanized cranberry (G)

galvanized satin-finish light smoky amethyst (H)

galvanized earth gold iris (I)

sparkling bright pink-lined clear (J)

light metallic lavender (K)

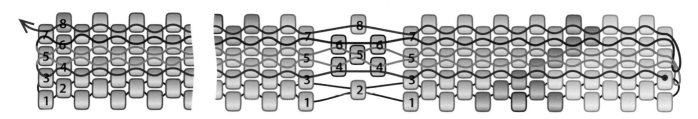

FIG. 2: Stitching Rows 4–8

ROW 15: Work 9 stitches with 1 bead in each stitch and 1 stitch with 2 beads. Work 8 stitches with 1 bead in each stitch and 1 stitch with 2 beads; repeat. Work 9 stitches with 1 bead in each stitch and 1 stitch with 2 beads; repeat. Work 8 stitches with 1 bead in each stitch and 1 stitch with 2 beads; repeat. Work 8 stitches with 1 bead in each stitch for a total of 81 beads in this row (**FIG. 3, BLACK THREAD**).

ROW 16: Work 80 stitches with 1 bead in each stitch, splitting the 2-bead sets of the previous row (**FIG. 3, YELLOW THREAD**).

ROW 17: Work 81 stitches with 1 bead in each stitch (**FIG. 3, PINK THREAD**).

ROW 18: Work 8 stitches with 1 bead in each stitch, then pass through the next bead of Row 17 to form a decrease. Work 9 stitches with 1 bead in each stitch, then form a decrease; repeat. Work 10 stitches with 1 bead in each stitch, then form a decrease; repeat. Work 9 stitches with 1 bead in each stitch, then form a decrease; repeat. Work 9 stitches with 1 bead in each stitch for a total of 73 beads in this row (**FIG. 3, PURPLE THREAD**). *NOTE: Allow the work to "bump" and curl into itself.*

ROW 19: Work 74 stitches with 1 bead in each stitch (**FIG. 3, ORANGE THREAD**).

ROW 20: Work 73 stitches with 1 bead in each stitch (**FIG. 3, GREEN THREAD**).

ROW 21: Work 8 stitches with 1 bead in each stitch, then pass through the next bead of Row 20 to form a decrease; repeat twice. Work 9 stitches with 1 bead in each stitch, then form a decrease; repeat. Work 8 stitches with 1 bead in each stitch, then form a decrease; repeat. Work 9 stitches with 1 bead in each stitch for a total of 67 beads in this row (**FIG. 3, BLUE THREAD**).

ROW 22: Work 66 stitches with 1 bead in each stitch. *NOTE: You will add 1 bead over the decreases of the previous row* (**FIG. 3, RED THREAD**).

ROWS 23–25: Repeat Rows 9–11.

ROW 26: Work 8 stitches with 1 bead in each stitch, then work 1 stitch with 2 beads. Work 7 stitches with 1 bead in each stitch, then work 1 stitch with 2 beads; repeat. Work 8 stitches with 1 bead in each stitch, then work 1 stitch with 2 beads; repeat. Work 7 stitches with 1 bead in each stitch, then work 1 stitch with 2 beads; repeat. Work 7 stitches with 1 bead in each stitch for a total of 73 beads in this row.

ROWS 27–31: Repeat Rows 5–9. Secure the thread and trim.

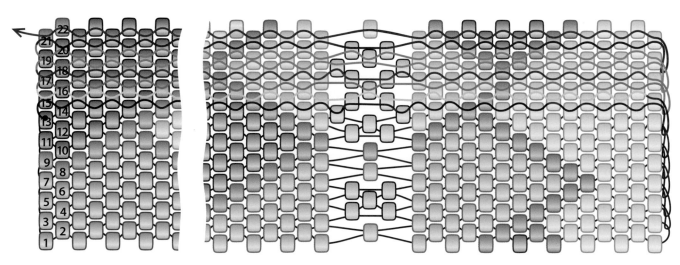

FIG. 3: Adding Rows 15–22

② Snap

Use brick stitch to form a tab, then sew on the snaps:

TAB ROW 1: Start 3' (0.9 m) of new conditioned thread that exits from the fourth bead at the edge of the base, away from the beadwork (the first bead of Row 7). String 2A, pass under the thread between edge beads of Rows 7 and 9, and pass back through the second A just added. String 1A, pass under the thread between edge beads of Rows 9 and 11, and pass back through the A just added. Continue working brick stitch, following the pattern in **FIG. 4**, for a total of 11 beads (**FIG. 4, GREEN THREAD**).

TAB ROWS 2–8: Continue working brick stitch to form a tab 8 rows long (**FIG. 4, BLUE THREAD**). Weave through beads to exit from the center of Tab Row 7, toward Row 6 (**FIG. 4, RED THREAD**).

SNAP: Check the bracelet for fit, then securely sew the male half of the snap to the inside of the tab just stitched. Start 12" (30.5 cm) of new conditioned thread at the other end of the base and sew the other half of the snap to the outside of the base. Secure all threads and trim.

ALTERNATE COLORWAY

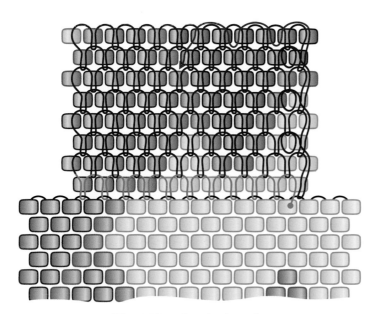

FIG. 4: Brick-stitching the clasp tab

Artist's Tip

- For a larger bracelet, simply add rows to the tab formed in Step 2.

Royal Countess

Regina Payne

techniques

Peyote stitch variation

Netting variation

materials

5 g metallic light gold bronze iris size 15° Japanese
seed beads (A)

0.5 g gilt-lined white opal size 11° Japanese
seed beads (B)

2 g higher metallic amethyst size 11° Japanese
cylinder beads (C)

2 g 24k gold-plated rainbow rose size 11° Japanese
cylinder beads (D)

66 crystal purple haze 3mm crystal bicones (E)

34 amethyst 3mm crystal bicones (F)

1 golden shadow 8mm crystal marguerite
lochrose flower

Smoke 6 lb FireLine braided beading thread

Microcrystalline wax

tools

Scissors

2 size 12 beading needles

finished size

6⅞" (17.5 cm)

① Bracelet

Use peyote stitch to form the base of the bracelet and a variation of netting to embellish it:

ROWS 1 AND 2: Place a needle at each end of 9' (2.7 m) of waxed thread. Use 1 needle to string 134C (**FIG. 1, PINK THREAD**); center the beads on the thread.

ROW 3: Use the right needle to work 67 peyote stitches with 1C in each stitch (**FIG. 1, ORANGE THREAD**).

ROWS 4 AND 5: Use the top needle to work 67 peyote stitches with 1D in each stitch off of Row 3 (**FIG. 1, PURPLE THREAD**); repeat using the bottom needle to work off of Row 1 (**FIG. 1, GREEN THREAD**).

ROWS 6 AND 7: Use the top needle to string 1D and pass back through the nearest D of Row 4, the next C of Row 3, and the following D of Row 4; repeat thirty-two times. String 1D; pass back through the next D of Row 4 (**FIG. 1, BLUE THREAD**). Use the bottom needle to repeat from the beginning of this row along the other edge (**FIG. 1, RED THREAD**).

CLASP BUTTON: Use the top needle to string 4A, the crystal flower, and 1A; pass back through the flower and the fourth A just added. String 3A; pass through the nearest D of Row 5 and the next D of Row 7 (**FIG. 2, PINK THREAD**). Use the bottom needle to repeat the thread path of the clasp button in reverse, exiting from the nearest D of Row 6 (**FIG. 2, ORANGE THREAD**).

ROWS 8 AND 9: Use the top needle to string 1A, 1E, and 1A and pass back through the next D of Row 6; repeat thirty-two times (**FIG. 2, PURPLE THREAD**). Use the bottom needle to repeat from the beginning of this row along the other edge (**FIG. 2, GREEN THREAD**).

CLASP LOOP: Use the top needle to string 20A or as many beads as needed to fit over the crystal flower, then pass through the nearest D of Row 7 and the following 1A/1E/1A (**FIG. 2, BLUE THREAD**). Use the bottom needle to repeat the thread path of the clasp loop in reverse (**FIG. 2, RED THREAD**).

ROWS 10 AND 11: Use the top needle to string 1A and pass back through the next 1A/1E/1A; repeat thirty times

(**FIG. 3, BLACK THREAD**). String 1A; pass through the next 1A/1E (**FIG. 3, PINK THREAD**). Use the bottom needle to repeat from the beginning of this row along the other edge (**FIG. 3, ORANGE THREAD**).

ROWS 12 AND 13: Use the top needle to string 4A and pass back through the nearest A of Row 10; repeat thirty-one times. String 4A; pass through the nearest A of Row 8 (**FIG. 3, PURPLE THREAD**). Use the bottom needle to repeat from the beginning of this row along the other edge (**FIG. 3, GREEN THREAD**). Use the top needle to weave through beads and exit back through the last 2A of the last 4A set along the opposite edge (**FIG. 3, BLUE THREAD**); repeat using the bottom needle (**FIG. 3, RED THREAD**).

ROWS 14 AND 15: Use the top needle to string 1A and pass through the next 2A of Row 12, 1A of Row 10, and 2A of Row 12; repeat thirty-one times. String 1A; pass through the next 2A of Row 12, then weave through beads to exit from the nearest D of Row 4 (**FIG. 4, BLACK THREAD**). Use the bottom needle to repeat from the beginning of this row along the other edge, exiting from the nearest D of Row 5 (**FIG. 4, TURQUOISE THREAD**).

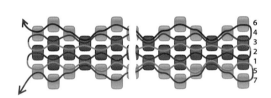

FIG. 1: Stitching Rows 1–7

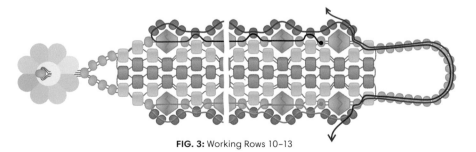

FIG. 2: Adding the clasp and Rows 8 and 9

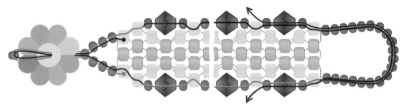

FIG. 3: Working Rows 10–13

ROW 16: Use the top needle to string 1A, 1F, and 2A; pass through the nearest E of Row 8 (**FIG. 4, PINK THREAD**). String 2A, 1F, and 2A and pass through the next E of Row 8; repeat thirty-one times (**FIG. 4, ORANGE THREAD**). String 2A, 1F, and 1A; pass through the nearest D of Row 6, toward the beadwork (**FIG. 4, PURPLE THREAD**).

ROW 17: Use the bottom needle to string 1A; pass through the nearest F of Row 16. String 2A; pass through the next E of Row 9 (**FIG. 4, GREEN THREAD**). String 2A and pass through the next F of Row 16, then string 2A and pass through the following E of Row 9; repeat thirty-one times (**FIG. 4, BLUE THREAD**). String 2A; pass through the nearest F of Row 16. String 1A; pass through the next D of Row 7, toward the beadwork (**FIG. 4, RED THREAD**). Use the top needle to pass back through the last A added by that needle and the last F added in Row 16.

ROW 18: String 1A, 1B, and 1A and pass back through the next F of Row 16 (**FIG. 5, BLUE THREAD**); repeat thirty-two times (**FIG. 5, RED THREAD**). Secure and trim this thread. Use the bottom needle to repeat the thread path of this row to reinforce. Secure and trim the thread.

Artist's Tips

- Adjust the size of the bracelet by adding or subtracting by 4 Delicas in the base band.

- To make a bangle, start with a number of Delicas in Rounds 1 and 2 that is divisible by four. At the end of Rounds 1 and 2, pass through the first bead strung to form a ring.

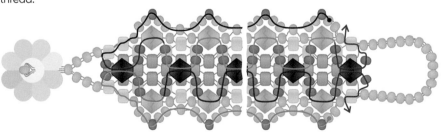

FIG. 4: Forming Rows 14–17

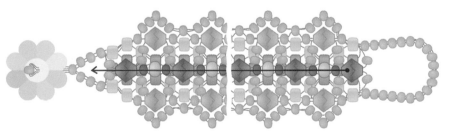

FIG. 5: Finishing Row 18

Line 'em Up

Christina Neit

techniques

Flat and circular peyote stitch

Netting

Right-angle weave

materials

1 g antiqued copper size 15° Japanese seed beads (A)

6 g bright copper size 11° metal seed beads (B)

4 g green-lined blue zircon iris size 11° Japanese seed beads (C)

5 g terra-cotta permanent finish size 8° Japanese seed beads (D)

45 crystal copper 5×2.5mm 2-hole seed beads (E)

48 teal suede 6mm flat 2-hole triangles (F)

1 antiqued silver 15mm hammered metal shank button

Smoke 8 lb braided beading thread

tools

Scissors

Size 11 beading needle

finished size

7¼" (18.5 cm)

① Base

Use a combination of beads and stitches to form the bracelet base:

ROW 1, FIRST PASS: Add a stop bead to the end of 6' (1.8 m) of thread, leaving a 4" (10 cm) tail. String {1B and 1F} forty-eight times, taking care that all of the F are pointing in the same direction. String 3B; pass through the second (bottom) hole of the last F added (**FIG. 1, BLUE THREAD**).

ROW 1, SECOND PASS: String 1B and pass through the bottom hole of the next F added in the first pass; repeat forty-seven times. String 2B; remove the stop bead and tie a knot with the working and tail threads to secure the work, then pass through the first B and the top hole of the first F added in the row (**FIG. 1, RED THREAD**).

ROW 2: String 1A, 1B, and 1A, then pass through the last F exited (top hole) and the following 1B/1F (top hole) of Row 1 to form a net; repeat to the end of the row, then weave through the nearest end 3B of Row 1 and the last F (bottom hole) of Row 1. String 1A, 1B, and 1A, then pass through the last F exited (bottom hole) and the following 1B/1F (bottom hole) of Row 1; repeat to the end of the row. Step up through the first 1A/1B of the final net (**FIG. 2**).

ROW 3: String 1D and pass through the next B of Row 2; repeat to the end of the row. Pass through the nearest A of Row 2, the end 3B of Row 1, and the next 1A/1B of Row 2. Repeat from the beginning of this row; weave through beads to exit from the first D added in this row (**FIG. 3, BLUE THREAD**).

ROW 4: String 1C and pass through the next D of Row 3; repeat to the end of the row, then weave through the beads along the end to exit from the first D on the other side of the work. Repeat from the beginning of this row; weave through beads to exit from the first C added in this row (**FIG. 3, RED THREAD**).

ROW 5, UNIT 1: String 3C, pass through the last C exited, the next D of Row 3, and the following C of Row 4 to form a right-angle weave unit (**FIG. 4, PURPLE THREAD**).

ROW 5, UNIT 2: String 2C; pass back through the nearest side C of the previous unit, through the last C exited, the next D of Row 3, and the following C of Row 4 (**FIG. 4, BLUE THREAD**).

ROW 5, UNITS 3 TO END: Repeat Unit 2 forty-four times. Weave through beads to exit from the first C added on the other side of Row 4. Repeat Row 5, Unit 1. Repeat Row 5, Unit 2 forty-five times. Weave through beads to exit from the second C added in this row, toward the center of the work (**FIG. 4, RED THREAD**).

ROW 6: Turn the beadwork so the points of the triangles face down and the working thread is at the top of the work. String 1E and pass through the top C of the next Row 5 unit; repeat forty-four times. Manipulate the E so that they sit on the

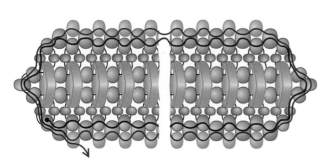

FIG. 1: Forming Row 1

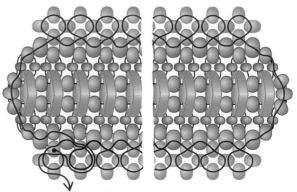

FIG. 2: Stitching Row 2

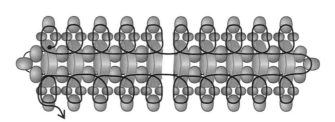

FIG. 3: Adding Rows 3 and 4

FIG. 4: Stitching Row 5

back of the beadwork (**FIG. 5, PURPLE THREAD**). String 3C; pass through the bottom C of the first Row 5 unit along the bottom edge of the beadwork and the second (bottom) hole of the nearest E (**FIG. 5, BLUE THREAD**). Pass through the bottom C of the next Row 5 unit along the bottom edge of the beadwork and the bottom hole of the next E; repeat forty-three times and pass through the bottom C of the final Row 5 unit. String 3C; pass through the top C of the first Row 5 unit. Weave through beads to exit from the first D of Row 3, toward the center of the work (**FIG. 5, RED THREAD**).

ROW 7: String 1C and pass through the next D of Row 3; repeat to the end of the row, then weave through beads to exit from the first D of Row 3 along the other edge of the beadwork. Repeat from the beginning of this step. Weave through beads to exit from the middle B of the 3B set added at the end of Row 1 (**FIG. 6**).

2 Clasp

Attach the button and use circular peyote stitch to form the clasp loop:

BUTTON: String 3C, the button, and 3C; pass through the last B exited (**FIG. 7, PURPLE THREAD**). Repeat the thread path several times to reinforce. Secure the threads and trim.

LOOP, ROUNDS 1 AND 2: Start 12" (30.5 cm) of new thread that exits from the middle B of the 3B set at the other end of Row 1. String 29C; pass through the last B exited and the first C just added (**FIG. 7, BLUE THREAD**). Test to see if the beads fit snugly around the button and adjust as needed, keeping an odd count.

LOOP, ROUND 3: String 1C, skip 1C of the previous round, and pass through the following C; repeat thirteen times. Pass through the nearest B (**FIG. 7, RED THREAD**). Secure the thread and trim.

Artist's Tips

- This bracelet is bead-type specific. It is important to use either Miyuki or Toho round seed beads and to use the metal beads where indicated. Cylindrical seed beads, such as Delicas, will not work.

- This bracelet can be made into a bangle by working rounds instead of rows of peyote stitch.

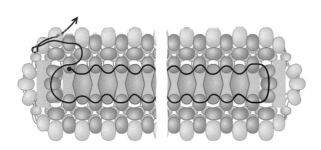

FIG. 5: Zipping the bracelet together with Row 6

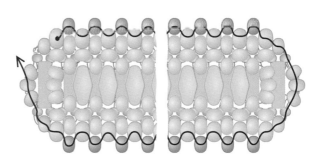

FIG. 6: Adding Row 7

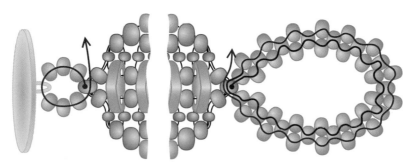

FIG. 7: Stitching the button-and-loop clasp

Inca Gold

Carole E. Hanley

techniques

Ladder stitch

Brick stitch

materials

3 g silver-lined gold size 11° cylinder beads (A)

5 g silver-lined brown size 11° cylinder beads (B)

2 g light yellow Ceylon size 11° cylinder beads (C)

2 g crystal-lined gray size 11° cylinder beads (D)

2 g crystal-lined salmon luster size 11° cylinder beads (E)

1 gold-plated 7×12mm lobster clasp

2" of gold-plated 3×4mm curb extension chain with charm

White size B Nymo nylon beading thread

tools

Scissors

Size 11 beading needle

finished size

7" [18 cm] (adjustable to 9" [23 cm])

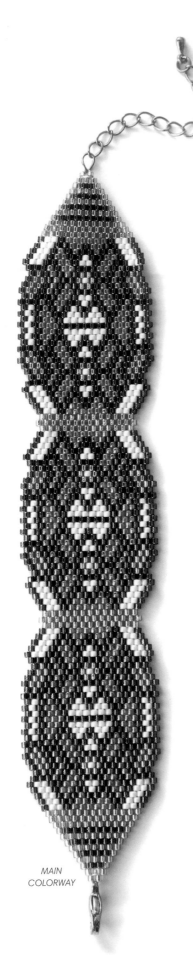

MAIN COLORWAY

① Band

Use ladder stitch and brick stitch to form the bracelet band:

ROW 1: Use 6' (1.8 cm) of thread to string 2A; pass through the beads again and exit the first A strung, leaving a 6" (15 cm) tail (**FIG. 1**).

ROW 2 (INCREASE): String 2A; pass under the exposed thread loop between the 2A of Row 1, then pass back through the last A added (**FIG. 2, BLUE THREAD**). String 1A; pass under the same exposed thread loop and back through the last A added (**FIG. 2, RED THREAD**).

ROW 3 (INCREASE): String 1A and 1B; pass under the nearest exposed thread loop and back through the last B added. String 1B; pass under the next exposed thread loop and back through the last B added. String 1A; pass under the same exposed thread loop as in the previous stitch and back through the last A added (**FIG. 3, BLUE THREAD**).

ROW 4 (INCREASE): String 2A; pass under the nearest exposed thread loop and back through the last A added. String 1A and pass under the next exposed thread loop and back through the last A added; repeat. String 1A; pass under the same exposed thread loop as in the previous stitch and back through the last A added (**FIG. 3, RED THREAD**).

ROWS 5–17 (INCREASES): Continue in brick stitch, following the pattern in **FIG. 4** to form increases. *NOTE: The last 2 stitches of each row will be formed in the same exposed thread loop.*

ALTERNATE COLORWAY

Artist's Tips

- Use medium tension so the bracelet remains flexible.

- Main colorway of bracelet shown uses the following Delica color numbers: DB42 for A, DB150 for B, DB203 for C, DB242 for D, and DB1325 for E.

ROW 18 (DECREASE): String 2B; skip the nearest exposed thread loop and pass under the next exposed thread loop. Pass back through the last B added (**FIG. 5, BLUE THREAD**). Pass back through the first 2B of this row to make the edge bead sit flat against the previous row (**FIG. 5, RED THREAD**). Continue brick-stitching the row as before, adding 1 bead to each exposed thread loop and following the pattern in **FIG. 4**. *NOTE: The last 2 stitches of decrease rows are not formed in the same exposed thread loop as when making increases* (**FIG. 6**).

ROWS 19-61: Continue in brick stitch, following the pattern in **FIG. 4**, to form increases and decreases. When working increase rows, follow the thread paths of Rows 3 and 4; when working decrease rows, follow the thread path of Row 18.

ROWS 62-95: Repeat Rows 28-61.

ROWS 96-107: Continue in brick stitch, following the pattern in **FIG. 4**, to form increases and decreases.

ROWS 108-123 (DECREASES): Continue in brick stitch, following the pattern in **FIG. 4**, to form decreases.

② Clasp

String the ring of the clasp and pass through the 2A of Row 123; repeat the thread path several times to reinforce. Secure the working thread and trim. Using the tail thread, repeat this entire step to attach the end of the chain that's opposite the charm to Row 1.

FIG. 1: Working Row 1

FIG. 2: Stitching Row 2

FIG. 3: Working Rows 3 and 4

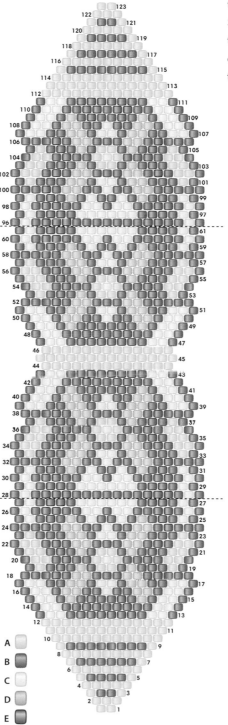

FIG. 4: Brick-stitch pattern

REPEAT ROWS 28-61 ONCE

FIG. 5: Forming a decrease at the start of Row 18

FIG. 6: Forming a decrease at the end of Row 18

40

Ilona

Yasmin Sarfati

techniques

Netting

Wireworking

materials

5 g metallic gold size 11° seed beads (A)

5 g metallic gold permanent-finish size 8° seed beads (B)

5 g opaque green luster 5×3mm 2-hole seed beads (C)

20 crystal 8mm (SS39) crystal chatons

6½" (16.5 cm) (20 setting links) of brass 8mm cup chain

1 gold-plated 14×20mm crystal-studded magnetic ball clasp

2 gold-plated 6mm jump rings

Gold nylon beading thread

tools

Scissors

Size 11 beading needle

2 pairs of chain- or flat-nose pliers

finished size

7" (18 cm)

1 Base

Use netting to stitch through the cup chain to form the bracelet base:

ROW 1: Use 6' (1.8 cm) of thread to pass up through the first setting on the cup chain, leaving a 3' (0.9 m) tail. *String 1B, 1C, and 3A; pass down through the second (right) hole of the C just added. String 1B; pass down through the next setting on the cup chain (**FIG. 1, GREEN THREAD**). String 1B, 1C, and 3A; pass up through the second (left) hole of the C just added. String 1B; pass up through the previous setting, then weave through beads to exit down through the next setting on the chain (**FIG. 1, BLUE THREAD**).** String 1B, 1C, and 3A; pass up through the right hole of the C just added. String 1B; pass up through the next setting on the cup chain. String 1B, 1C, and 3A; pass down through the left hole of the C just added. String 1B; pass down through the previous setting, then weave through beads to exit up through the following setting (**FIG. 1, RED THREAD**). Repeat from * eight times, then repeat from * to ** for a total of 19 nets on each side of the chain.

CLASP LOOP: String 12A and pass down through the last setting exited (**FIG. 2, BLUE THREAD**); repeat the thread path to reinforce. Pass through the nearest 1B/1C(right hole)/3A/1C(left hole)/1B, the previous setting, and the following 1B/1C(left hole)/1A (**FIG. 2, RED THREAD**).

ROW 2: String 1C and 3A; pass down through the left hole of the C just added, the nearest A of the next 3A set of Row 1, and the right hole of the following C, then pass up through the left hole of the same C and the nearest A of the 3A set (**FIG. 3**). Repeat from the beginning of this row seventeen times for a total of 18 nets. Secure the working thread and trim.

Add a needle to the tail thread and repeat the clasp loop and Row 2 on the other edge of Row 1.

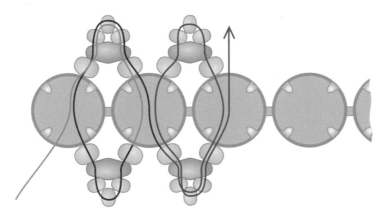

FIG. 1: Beginning Row 1 of the base

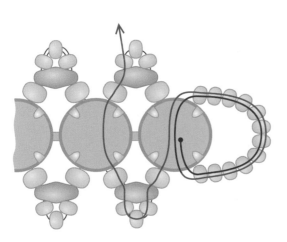

FIG. 2: Adding the first clasp loop

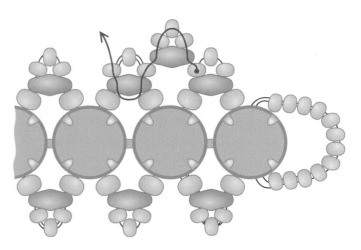

FIG. 3: Forming the first stitch of Row 2

② Stones

Place 1 chaton into 1 setting link of the chain and use the pliers to fold all 4 prongs over the edges of the chaton to secure it in place; repeat nineteen times using the remaining chatons and setting links.

③ Clasp

Use 1 jump ring to attach one half of the clasp to one clasp loop; repeat to add the second half of the clasp to the other clasp loop.

Artist's Tip

- If you can't find cup chain, you may use 8mm crystal montées.

ALTERNATE COLORWAY

MAIN COLORWAY

Primrose Path

Jennifer and Susan G. Schwartzenberger

techniques

Netting

Wireworking

materials

3 g matte metallic light olive size 15° seed beads (A)

2 g gold-lined crystal size 11° seed beads (B)

5 g chalk white luster 5×3mm 2-hole seed beads (C)

34 dark powder rose 6mm glass pearls (D)

1 brass 7×12mm lobster clasp with 4mm jump ring

1 brass 5.5mm jump ring

2 brass wireguards

Olive size D nylon beading thread

Thread conditioner

tools

Scissors

Size 10 beading needle

2 pairs of chain- or flat-nose pliers

finished size

8⅛" (20.5 cm)

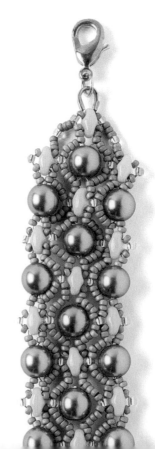

① Row 1

Use netting to form the center row of the bracelet:

STITCH 1: Use 4' (1.2 m) of thread to string 1C, 1A, 1B, 1A, the second (right) hole of the C just added, 1A, 1B, and 1A, leaving an 8" (20.5 cm) tail; pass up through the first (left) hole of the C, through the first 1A/1B/1A, and down through the right hole of the C (**FIG. 1, GREEN THREAD**).

STITCH 2: String 2A, 1D, 2A, 1C, 1A, 1B, 1A, the right hole of the C just added, 1A, 1B, and 1A; pass down through the left hole of the C just added (**FIG. 1, BLUE THREAD**). String 2A; pass back through the D. String 2A; pass down through the right hole of the C in the previous stitch and through the first 2A of this stitch (**FIG. 1, RED THREAD**).

STITCH 3: String 4A, 1B, and 4A; pass back through the nearest 2A of the previous stitch, up through the left hole of the nearest C, and back through the next 2A of the previous stitch (**FIG. 2, BLUE THREAD**). String 4A, 1B, and 4A; pass through the D of the previous stitch and weave through beads to exit down through the right hole of the C in the previous stitch (**FIG. 2, RED THREAD**).

STITCHES 4 AND ON: Repeat Stitches 2 and 3 eleven times or to the desired length minus 1" (2.5 cm) for the clasp. Weave through beads to exit from the last B added in the final stitch, toward the beadwork.

② Row 2

Continue to use netting to stitch the second row of the bracelet:

STITCH 1: String 1A, 1C, 1A, 1B, and 1A; pass down through the right hole of the C just added. String 1A; pass through the last B exited in Row 1, the first A of this stitch, and up through the left hole of the following C (**FIG. 3, GREEN THREAD**).

STITCH 2: String 2A, 1D, 2A, 1C, 1A, 1B, 1A, the left hole of the C just added, and 1A; pass back through the B over the top of the next D in Row 1. String 1A; pass up through the right hole of the last C added (**FIG. 3, BLUE THREAD**). String 2A; pass back through the last D added. String 2A; pass up through the left hole of the C in the previous stitch, the first 2A/1D added in this stitch, the nearest 2A at the top of this stitch, down through the right hole of the C added in this stitch, and back through the nearest 2A at the bottom of this stitch (**FIG. 3, RED THREAD**).

STITCH 3: String 4A; pass through the nearest B of Row 1. String 4A; pass through the nearest 2A at the bottom of the previous stitch and up through the left hole of the nearest C (**FIG. 4, BLUE THREAD**). Weave through beads to exit up through the left hole of the next C (**FIG. 4, RED THREAD**).

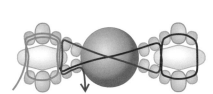

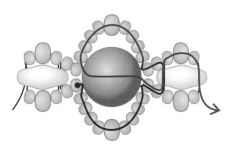

FIG. 1: Forming Stitches 1 and 2 of Row 1

FIG. 2: Adding Stitch 3 of Row 1

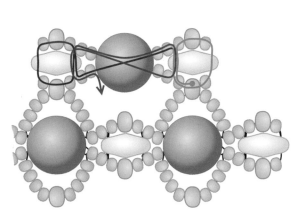

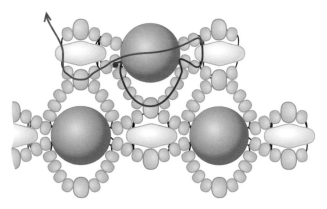

FIG. 3: Working Stitches 1 and 2 of Row 2

FIG. 4: Adding Stitch 3 of Row 2

STITCHES 4 AND ON: Repeat Stitches 2 and 3 ten times or to the end of Row 1. Weave through beads to exit from the first B of Row 1, Stitch 3, toward the beadwork.

③ Row 3

Rotate the beadwork 180 degrees. Repeat Row 2. Weave through beads to exit up through the end A at the bottom of the final C in this row.

④ Clasp

Connect the clasp to the bracelet:

TOP BRIDGE: String 3A, 1B, and 3A; pass back through the B over the top of the end C in Row 1, the following A, and the left hole of the C (**FIG. 5, GREEN THREAD**).

WIREGUARD: String 1 wireguard, then pass down through the last C exited; repeat the thread path to reinforce. Pass back through the following 1A/1B (**FIG. 5, BLUE THREAD**).

BOTTOM BRIDGE: String 3A, 1B, and 3A; pass through the end A of Row 2 (currently on the top left of the end C in Row 2) (**FIG. 5, RED THREAD**). Secure the working thread and trim.

CLASP: Attach the clasp, via the jump ring, to the previous wireguard.

Add a needle to the tail thread. Repeat this entire step at the other end of the bracelet, attaching the jump ring to the second wireguard.

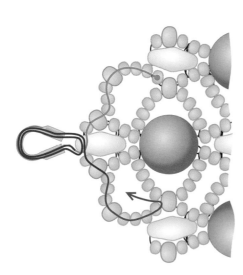

FIG. 5: Connecting a wireguard and forming the bridges

Artist's Tips

- If the two-hole seed bead holes are plugged, remove any blockage with the tip of a fine-tip awl or discard the bead.

- If just one hole of a two-hole seed bead is blocked, you can set the bead aside and use it as a drop in another project.

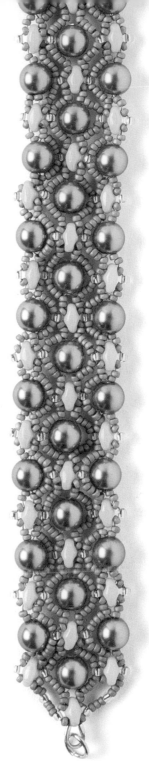

MAIN COLORWAY

Edgy Kumihimo

Sue Charette-Hood

techniques

Kumihimo braiding

Wireworking

materials

20 g berry-lined dark amethyst size 8° Japanese seed beads (A)

144 or more matte purple 4×7mm long drops (B)

2 purple velvet 8mm crystal bicones

2 metallic purple 14×9mm faceted large-hole glass rondelles with steel grommets

14" (35.5 cm) of sterling silver 20-gauge wire

Moss green 40 lb braided beading thread

tools

Scissors

Large-eye beading needle

1–2 oz fishing weight

Kumihimo braiding disc

Wire cutters

Flat-nose pliers

Round-nose pliers

finished size

9" (23 cm)

1 Preparation

String the beads and prepare for braiding:

STRANDS: Form a wrapped loop at the end of one 8" (20.5 cm) piece of wire. *NOTE: The loop must be small enough to fit inside a large-hole bead when assembling the bracelet.* Cut four 42" (106.5 cm) strands of thread. Center the 4 threads in the wrapped loop and knot the threads around the loop.

STRINGING: Place the large-eye needle at the end of 1 strand and string 50A; secure the beads with a stop bead near the end of the strand. Repeat three times for a total of 4 strands with 50A on each. Repeat four times using B for a total of 4 strands with 40B on each.

DISC SETUP: Slide the beads toward the stop bead on each strand. Holding the kumihimo disc with the numbered side up, insert the straight end of the wire down through the disc's center hole.

Gently bend the end of the wire into a U and hook the weight onto it. Distribute the 8 strands as shown in Kumihimo Braiding 101 (**FIG. A**). Slide the stop bead up each strand until the first bead is 2" (5 cm) below the disc.

2 Braid

To start, follow the kumihimo braiding pattern shown in **FIGURES B AND C** in Kumihimo Braiding 101 eight times without adding beads. For the ninth and subsequent repeats, bring the top bead on each strand to the hole in the center of the disc. Slide the bead under the nearest strand that is crossed to the right or left; this locks each bead in place. After each turn, check the tension and bead position on the braid. Continue braiding until the beaded section is about 1" (2.5 cm) shorter than your wrist measurement.

3 Finishing

Complete the braid, secure the beaded section, and make the clasp:

FINAL ROUNDS: Remove the stop beads and remaining beads from the 8 strands. Lay one 6" (15 cm) piece of wire across the center hole, on top of the disc. Continue braiding without beads above the wire for eight repeats. Remove 2 strands from opposing slots on the disc and knot them over the wire. Repeat three times to knot the remaining 6 strands.

EYE HALF OF CLASP: Slide the knots to 2" (5 cm) from one end of the wire and form a small wrapped loop that includes the knots in the loop. *NOTE: The loop must be small enough to fit inside a large-hole bead.* Gather the 8 strands, knot them, and trim them close to the knot. Use the wrapped-loop wire to string 1 large-hole bead, 1 bicone, and 1A, hiding the end of the braid and knots inside the large-hole bead; form a wrapped loop at least ⅜" (1 cm) in diameter (**FIG 1**).

HOOK HALF OF CLASP: Remove the braid from the disc, take the weight off the bent wire, and straighten the wire. Use the wire to string 1 large-hole bead, 1 bicone, and 1A, hiding the end of the braid and knots inside the large-hole bead. Use flat-nose pliers to grasp the wire 1¼" (3.2 cm) from the A and fold the wire back onto itself. Use the tail to form a wrap just above the A. Bend the folded end toward the bracelet to form a hook (**FIG. 2**).

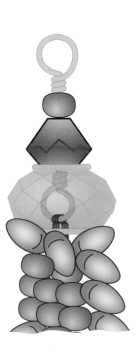

FIG. 1: Forming the eye half of the clasp

FIG. 2: Making the hook half of the clasp

Kumihimo Braiding 101

① Hold the disc parallel to the floor with number 32 held away from you. Tuck the strands into the slots around the disc and place the wire through the center hole (**FIG. A**). *NOTE: See* **FIG. A** *caption for specific positioning of strands for this design.* Adding a weight to the wire below the disc helps keep the correct tension. The braid will form at the center hole, extending below the disc as you work. Do not allow the strands to tangle and keep the weight suspended.

② Move the bottom left strand between notches 16 and 17 up to the notch between 30 and 31. Move the top right strand between notches 32 and 1 down to the notch between 14 and 15 (**FIG. B**). Rotate the disc one-quarter turn clockwise so number 24 is now at the farthest (top) position where number 32 used to be (**SHOWN AT THE TOP OF FIG. C**).

③ Move the bottom left strand between notches 8 and 9 up to the notch between notches 22 and 23. Move the top right strand between notches 24 and 25 down to the notch between 6 and 7 (**FIG. C**). Rotate the disc one-quarter turn clockwise.

④ Using the strands that are now the farthest and closest to you after the turn, repeat Steps 2 and 3 until the braid is the desired length.

⑤ When making beaded braids, slide each bead to the center hole and tuck it firmly under the strand that crosses to the right or left to lock the bead in place. Do not allow the bead to pop up.

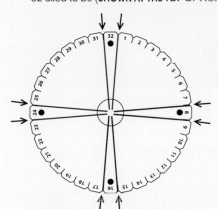
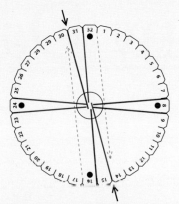
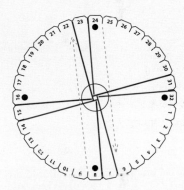

FIG. A: Load 1 strand with B beads into each of these slots: 23/24, 24/25, 31/32, and 32/1 (red thread). Load 1 strand with A beads into each of these slots: 7/8, 8/9, 15/16, and 16/17 (blue thread).

FIG. B: Moving the first two strands. The dotted green line shows the strand's movement from its starting point to its new position. New positions also marked by black arrows.

FIG. C: Moving the second two strands after making the quarter turn. The dotted green line shows the strand's movement from its starting point to its new position. After the next quarter-turn, number 15 will be at the farthest (top) position.

Artist's Tips

- Instead of making your own clasp, form wrapped loops at both ends of the bracelet and use jump rings to attach a clasp.

- Cut the beading thread longer than you think you'll need to avoid running short while braiding.

- No need to be exact with the number of beads you put on each strand. You can easily add or subtract beads as you work.

- Keep the weight in the center of the disc's hole. You may need to reposition the weight with your fingers until you get used to applying the right amount of tension when moving the threads.

- Let gravity help position the beads: Tilt the disc toward you when moving the upper strands and away from you for the lower strands.

- For convenience, place your kumihimo disc on top of a tall vase and let the weight hang inside while the strands hang outside around the edge.

- When making the final wrapped loops, wrap the wire very close to the end seed bead until the components are tight and do not move. This keeps the knots hidden inside the end bead.

Sunny Day

Carmella Patzlaff

techniques

Ladder stitch

Tubular herringbone stitch

Picot

Wireworking

materials

20 g matte galvanized green/teal permanent finish size 11° seed beads (A)

5 g blush marbled Dijon size 11° seed beads (B)

3 g red size 11° cylinder beads (C)

2 g silver-lined lichen size 8° seed beads (D)

2 g matte Picasso size 6° seed beads in olive, brown, teal, red, and blue (E)

8 bronze marbled turquoise 6mm Czech flat 2-hole squares (F)

1 bronze 5×9mm round magnetic clasp

2 bronze 4×6mm oval jump rings

1" (2.5 cm) of bronze 2–3×3–6mm long-and-short chain

Smoke 6 lb braided beading thread

Thread conditioner

tools

Scissors

Size 10 beading needle

2 pairs of chain- or flat-nose pliers

finished size

7½" (19 cm)

① Body

Work ladder and tubular herringbone stitches to form the bracelet's body:

BASE: Use 6' (1.8 m) of conditioned thread to form a ladder-stitched strip 4F long, leaving a 12" (30.5 cm) tail (**FIG. 1**). Fold the ladder to form a rectangle and stitch the first and fourth F together; exit from one of the rectangle's corners (**FIG. 2**).

ROUND 1: String 2A, pass down through the second hole of this F and up through the first hole of the next F; repeat three times. Step up through the first A added in this round (**FIG. 3, SHOWN FLAT FOR CLARITY**).

ROUND 2: String 2A, pass down through the next A from the previous round, down through the nearest hole from the F below, and up through the nearest hole of the next F and the following A of the previous round; repeat three times. Step up through the first A added in this round (**FIG. 4, GREEN THREAD**).

ROUND 3: String 2A; pass down through the next A of the previous round. String 1E; pass up through the following A of the previous round. String 2A; pass down through the next A of the previous round. String 1D; pass up through the following A of the previous round. Repeat from the beginning of this round. Step up through the first A added in this round (**FIG. 4, BLUE THREAD**). *NOTE: Alternate the colors of E throughout the project as desired.*

ROUND 4: String 2A; pass down through the next A, through the nearest E, and up through the following A of the previous round. String 2A; pass down through the next A, through the nearest D, and up through the following A of the previous round. Repeat from the beginning of this round. Step up through the first A added in this round (**FIG. 4, RED THREAD**).

ROUND 5: Repeat Round 3, adding 2B between herringbone-stitched columns over the E of Round 3 (the wide sides of the rope) and 1B between the columns over the D (the narrow sides) (**FIG. 5, PURPLE THREAD**).

ROUND 6: Repeat Round 3, adding 2C between columns on the wide sides and 1C between columns on the narrow sides (**FIG. 5, YELLOW THREAD**).

ROUND 7: Repeat Round 3, adding 2B between columns on the wide sides and 1B between columns on the narrow sides (**FIG. 5, GREEN THREAD**).

ROUND 8: Repeat Round 3, adding 1E between columns on the wide sides and 1D between columns on the narrow sides (**FIG. 5, BLUE THREAD**).

ROUND 9: Repeat Round 4 (**FIG. 5, RED THREAD**). *NOTE: To ensure a tight rope, when you're passing through the previous round's 1E, join it with the mirror E in the same round using a ladder stitch. There's no need to do this every round, but doing so every fourth repeat will help flatten the rope, establish the wide and narrow sides, and create a sturdy bracelet.*

FIG. 1: Ladder-stitching the base row

FIG. 2: Completing the base

FIG. 3: Adding Round 1

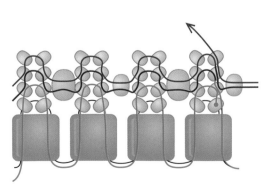

FIG. 4: Stitching Rounds 2–4

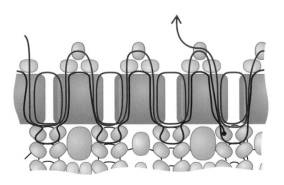

FIG. 6: Adding the end and picot rounds

Repeat Rounds 5–9 sixteen times, then repeat Rounds 5–8. *NOTE: To form a longer bracelet, stitch to the desired length, ending with a Round 8 repeat and keeping in mind that the clasp and other end will add 1" (2.5 cm) to the finished length.* Weave through beads to exit up through 1A before 1E.

② Finishing

Stitch the end round, then add picots and a clasp:

END ROUND: String 1F, pass down through the second hole of the F and the next A of the previous round, then pass up through the following A; repeat three times. Pass up through the first hole of the first F added in this round (**FIG. 6, BLUE THREAD**).

PICOTS: String 1B, 1A, and 1B and pass down through the next hole of the F below, up through the first hole of the following F, down through the nearest hole of the previous F, and up through the first hole of the next F; repeat three times. Weave through beads to exit from the first A added in this round (**FIG. 6, RED THREAD**).

CLASP: String 1A, one half of the clasp, and 1A, then pass through the last A exited to form a loop; repeat the thread path twice to reinforce and exit through the clasp (**FIG. 7, BLUE THREAD**). String 1A and pass through the A on the opposite side of the picot round, then string 1A and pass through the clasp; repeat this thread path twice to reinforce (**FIG. 7, RED THREAD**). Secure the working thread and trim. Use the tail thread to add picots and the second half of the clasp to the other end of the bracelet.

SAFETY CHAIN: Use 1 jump ring to connect 1 end of the chain to the loop of one half of the clasp. Use 1 jump ring to connect the other end of the chain to the second half of the clasp.

MAIN COLORWAY

Artist's Tip

- Be sure to begin and end your bracelet with size 6° seed beads between columns on the wide sides.

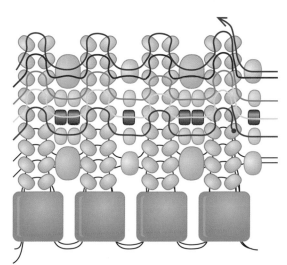

FIG. 5: Forming Rounds 5–9

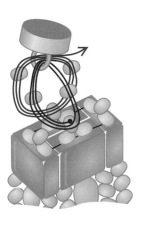

FIG. 7: Connecting the clasp

Heart-to-Heart

Janet Palumbo

techniques
Right-angle weave

Peyote stitch

Netting

materials
1 g purple hematite metallic size 15° seed beads (A)

14 g magic lilac 4×2mm Czech farfalle beads (B)

6 rosaline 3mm crystal pearl rounds (C)

5 rosaline 4mm crystal pearl rounds (D)

6 deep amethyst 6mm fire-polished rounds (E)

Smoke 6 lb braided beading thread

Thread conditioner

tools
Scissors

Size 11 or 12 beading needle

Thread burner (optional)

finished size
7½" (19 cm)

① Hearts

Use right-angle weave and peyote stitch to form a heart shape:

ROW 1: Use 5' (1.5 m) of conditioned thread and B to work a strip of right-angle weave 16 units wide, leaving a 2½' (0.8 m) tail so the first unit is at the center of the thread. Exit from the top bead of the final unit (**SEE THE BOTTOM STRIP OF FIG. 1 FOR ORIENTATION**).

ROW 2, UNITS 1 AND 2: String 3B; pass through the last B exited, the 3B just added, and the top B of Unit 15 in Row 1. String 2B; pass through the last 2B exited and the first B just added (**FIG. 1, BLUE THREAD**).

ROW 2, UNITS 3–16: String 3B; pass through the last B exited and the first 2B just added; repeat thirteen times (**FIG. 1, RED THREAD**). *NOTE: Just the first 2 units in this row are connected to Row 1.* Secure the working thread and trim. Add a needle to the tail thread and weave through beads to exit toward the work from the top bead of Unit 1, Row 1.

INNER SHAPING: *Pass through the top B of each of the next 6 Row 1 units, pulling tightly to force the work to curve. String 1A; pass through the top B of the next 2 Row 1 units. String 1A and pass through the next top B; repeat once. String 2A and pass through the next top B; repeat twice** (**FIG. 2, GREEN THREAD**).

String 1C; pass through the bottom B of Row 2, Unit 3 (**FIG. 2, BLUE THREAD**). Shape Row 2 by repeating this step from * to ** in reverse, working off of the bottom B of each unit. Weave through beads to exit from the top B of Row 2, Unit 16 (**FIG. 2, RED THREAD**).

OUTER SHAPING: String 1D; pass through the top B of the next Row 2 unit. String 2A and pass through the top B of the next Row 2 unit; repeat eight times. String 1A and pass through the top B of the next Row 2 unit; repeat twice (**FIG. 3, BLUE THREAD**). Weave through beads to exit from the mirror B at the bottom of Row 1.

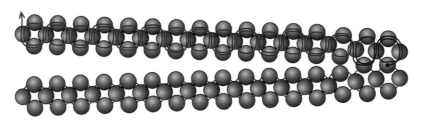

FIG. 1: Stitching the heart base

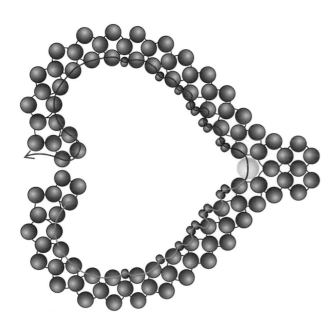

FIG. 2: Shaping the inner edge of the heart

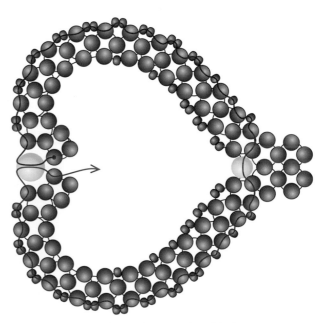

FIG. 3: Shaping the outer edge of the heart

Repeat the entire embellishment sequence in reverse, working off of the bottom B of each Row 1 unit, except in the final stitch, pass back through the D added at the beginning of this section instead of adding a new D, pulling tightly to connect the 2 heart halves (**FIG. 3, RED THREAD**).

CENTER: String 1B; pass through the nearest B of Row 2. Pass through the D and the next outside B of Row 2. String 1A; pass through the nearest B of Row 1. Pass back through the D and through the first B exited in this section (**FIG. 4**). Don't trim the thread; set aside.

Repeat this entire step to form a second heart.

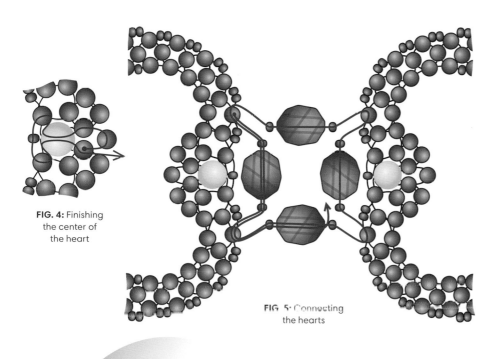

FIG. 4: Finishing the center of the heart

FIG. 5: Connecting the hearts

Artist's Tips

• Czech farfalle beads are not completely uniform. Discard those beads that are wafer-thin, and set aside 4 to 6 of the widest ones to use in the clasp ring.

• For this bracelet, the designer prefers the colors and finishes available in the Czech farfalle beads, but Japanese peanut beads can be substituted. Japanese berry beads are larger, so if using them, add only 3 units to the strips and 8 units to the clasp ring.

• For a dramatic choker necklace, add enough right-angle-weave units to the clasp strips between the ovals and the clasp halves.

MAIN COLORWAY

② Center Connection

Stitch the 2 hearts together:

BASE: Place the 2 hearts together so their tops touch. Weave the thread of the left heart through beads to exit from the top B of Unit 14, Row 2, toward the center of the heart. *String 1A, 1E, and 1A; pass through the mirror top B on the other side of the same heart. String 1A, 1E, 1A; pass up through the mirror B of the right heart. Repeat from *, then repeat the thread path to reinforce. Exit from the second E added in this section (**FIG. 5**).

NETTING: String 5A, 1D, and 5A; pass through the top E of the base. String 5A; pass back through the D just added. String 5A; pass through the original E exited (**FIG. 6, GREEN THREAD**). **String 2A; pass through the closest outside B of Row 1, Unit 4, of the right heart. String 1A, 1D, and 1A; pass through the mirror outside B of the left heart. String 2A; pass through the last E exited. Weave through beads to exit from the 1A/1D just added (**FIG. 6, PURPLE THREAD**). String 6A; pass through the last D exited and the first 3A just added. String 1A; pass through the next 3A and through the D again (**FIG. 6, BLUE THREAD**). Weave through beads to

exit from the top E of the base (**FIG. 6, RED THREAD**). Repeat from ** to embellish the other side of the base. Secure the working thread and trim. To tighten, add a needle to the tail thread and weave through all the A placed around each E. Secure the tail thread and trim. Set aside.

③ Ovals

Use right-angle weave and peyote stitch to form an oval component off of one of the hearts:

BASE: Repeat Step 1, Rows 1 and 2, this time forming just 10 units in each row. Don't trim the thread.

ATTACH: Flip the work to exit down through the end B of the last unit. String 1B; pass up through an end B of the bottom row at the base of the right heart. String 1B; pass down through the last B exited on the oval base. Weave through beads to exit from the second B added in this section and continue through the end bead in the other row of the oval base. String 1B; pass down through the end B of the top row at the base of the right heart, the second B added in this section, and the 4B in the last unit of the oval base (**FIG. 7, GREEN THREAD**).

INNER SHAPING: String 1C; pass through the next B on the inside of the oval. String 1A and pass through the next inside B; repeat twice. Pass through the next inside B. String 1A and pass through the next inside B; repeat twice. Pull tight to shape the oval. Repeat this entire section to shape the inside-bottom edge of the oval. Weave through beads to exit from the outside B of the last unit at the bottom of the oval (**FIG. 7, BLUE THREAD**).

OUTER SHAPING: String 1A; pass through the next outside B. String 2A and pass through the next outside B; repeat four times. String 1A; pass through the next outside B. Weave through beads to exit from the mirror B on the other side of the oval. Repeat this entire section to shape the top of the oval. Weave through the beads to exit from the bottom of the oval (**FIG. 7, RED THREAD**). Secure the working thread and trim, but leave the tail thread.

Repeat this entire step to add an oval to the base of the left heart.

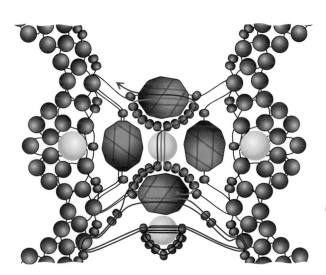

FIG. 6: Embellishing the heart connection with netting

FIG. 7: Adding the oval to the heart

ALTERNATE COLORWAY

④ Clasp Loop

Use right-angle weave to form the clasp loop:

STRIP: Add a needle to the left oval's tail thread and weave through beads to exit from the end B in the bottom row on the other end of the oval. String 1B; pass through the end B of the first unit in the top row of the left oval, and weave through beads to exit back through the B just added (**FIG. 8, PURPLE THREAD**). Repeat the thread path to reinforce. Use B to right-angle-weave 5 units; exit from a top B (**FIG. 8, GREEN THREAD**). *NOTE: You may add or subtract units here to size the bracelet.*

RING: Use the largest B (see the first Artist's Tip on page 209) to right-angle-weave 10 units. String 1B; pass through the B on the other side of the last strip unit. String 1B; pass through the end B of the tenth unit just formed (Fig. 8, blue thread). Weave through the 12B at the center of the ring to lightly gather the center (**FIG. 8, RED THREAD**). *NOTE: Use medium thread tension, or the ring might be too tight.* Don't trim the thread.

⑤ Clasp Fringe

Add a fringed toggle:

STRIP: Repeat the strip in Step 4 on the right oval, adding more or fewer units for fit.

FRINGE 1: String 18A, 1E, and 1A; pass back through the E and the next 15A. String 3A; pass through the end B (**FIG. 9**). Repeat the thread path to reinforce.

FRINGE 2: String 8A, 1E, and 1A; pass back through the E and the next 5A. String 3A; pass through the end B. Repeat the thread path to reinforce. Check the fit of the E through the clasp ring; tighten or loosen the clasp ring as necessary. Secure and trim all threads.

To wear, push the fringes, one at a time, through the clasp ring.

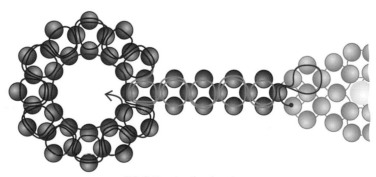

FIG. 8: Forming the clasp loop

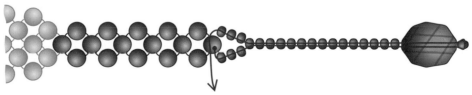

FIG. 9: Stitching the clasp's first fringe

Indian Summer

Susan Severs Council

techniques

Netting

Daisy chain variation

materials

2 g matte metallic citrine green iris or bronze size 11° seed beads (A)

5 g metallic bronze size 8° seed beads (B)

5 g opaque cream champagne luster 5×2.5mm 2-hole seed beads (C)

12 g hematite turquoise luster 5×2.5mm 2-hole seed beads (D)

24 cream 2.8mm Japanese drops (E)

21 opaque rose-gold luster topaz 6mm pressed-glass rounds (F)

1 antiqued gold 13×26mm magnetic foldover clasp

Smoke 8 lb braided beading thread

tools

Scissors

Size 10 beading needle

finished size

7½" (19 cm)

① Body

Working with tight tension, use a daisy chain variation and netting to form the bracelet's body:

PREPARE: Tie a stop bead to 6'(1.8 m) of thread, leaving a 12" (30.5 cm) tail.

ROW 1, UNIT 1: String 1B and 1F. String {1C and 1A} twice. String 1C; pass through the F just added (**FIG. 1, BLUE THREAD**). String {1C and 1A} twice. String 1C; pass through the F. String 1A and 1F (**FIG. 1, RED THREAD**).

ROW 1, UNIT 2: String 1A and 1F. String {1C and 1A} twice. String 1C; pass through the F just added. String {1C and 1A} twice. String 1C; pass through the F. String 1A and 1F (**FIG. 2, GREEN THREAD**).

ROW 1, UNITS 3–10: Repeat Row 1, Unit 2 eight times (**FIG. 2, BLUE THREAD**).

ROW 1, UNIT 11: String 1A and 1F. String {1C and 1A} twice. String 1C; pass through the F just added. String {1C and 1A} twice. String 1C; pass through the F.

String 3B; pass through the second hole of the nearest C along the top of the chain (**FIG. 2, RED THREAD**).

ROW 2: String 1D, 1B, and 1D; then pass through the second hole of the next C in Row 1; repeat (**FIG. 3, ORANGE THREAD**). *Pass through the nearest F and the second hole of the next C in Row 1; then pass through the second hole of the last D added (**FIG. 3, PURPLE THREAD**). String 1B and 1D; then pass through the second hole of the next C in Row 1. String 1D, 1B, and 1D; pass through the second hole of the following C in Row 1. Repeat from * eight times (**FIG. 3, GREEN THREAD**). Pass through the nearest F and the second hole of the next C in Row 1; then pass through the second hole of the last D added. String 1B and 1D; pass through the second hole of the next C in Row 1. String 1D, 1B, and 1D; pass through the second hole of the following C in Row 1 (**FIG. 3, BLUE THREAD**).

ROW 2 END: Remove the stop bead. String 2B; pass through the 1B/1F/1A at the beginning of Row 1. Loop the thread between beads to form a turnaround;

then pass back through the last 1A/1F/1B exited. String 2B; pass through the second hole of the end C on the other side of Row 1 (**FIG. 3, RED THREAD**).

ROW 3: Repeat Row 2 along the bottom of the work.

ROW 3 END: String 2B; pass back through the 1B nearest the final F of Row 1. Weave through beads to exit from the 3B added at the end of Row 1 and through the nearest top 1C (second hole)/1D (first hole)/1B/1D (first hole)/1C (second hole)/1D (first hole)/1B (**FIG. 4, ORANGE THREAD**).

ROW 4: String 1D, 1A, and 1D and pass through the nearest top 1B/1D (first hole)/1C (second hole)/1D (first hole)/1B; repeat nine times. Weave through beads to exit from the first 2B added at the end of Row 2 (**FIG. 4, GREEN THREAD**).

ROW 4 END: String 1B; pass through the next 2B at the end of Row 2 and through the nearest bottom 1C (second hole)/1D (first hole)/1B/1D (first hole)/1C (second hole)/1D (first hole)/1B.

FIG. 1: Forming Row 1, Unit 1

FIG. 2: Completing Row 1

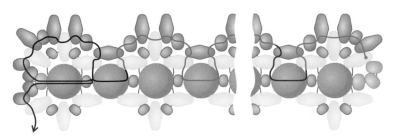

FIG. 3: Adding Row 2 and the Row 2 end

ROW 5: Repeat Row 4, exiting from the 2B added at the end of Row 3.

ROW 5 END: String 1B; pass through the next 2B at the end. String 1B; pass through the second hole of the nearest D (**FIG. 4, BLUE THREAD**).

ROW 6: String 1B, 1E, and 1B; pass through the second hole of the next D in Row 2. String 1B; pass through the second hole of the following D in Row 2 and the second hole of the nearest D in Row 4. **String 1B, 1E, and 1B; pass through the second hole of the next D in Row 4 and the second hole of the next D in Row 2. String 1B; pass through the second hole of the following D in Row 2 and the second hole of the nearest D in Row 4. Repeat from ** nine times. String 1B, 1E, and 1B; pass through the second hole of the next D in Row 2.

ROW 6 END: String 1B and pass through the next 2B at the end; repeat. String 1B; pass through the second hole of the nearest D in Row 3.

ROW 7: Repeat Row 6, working off of Row 5. String 1B; pass through the nearest B of the Row 3 end (**FIG. 4, RED THREAD**).

② Clasp

String 1B; pass up through one side of one half of the clasp and down through the other side. String 1B; pass through the second B added in the Row 5 end, back through the B just added, and back up through one side of the clasp. Pass down through the other side of the clasp, back through the first B added for the clasp, and through the original B (**FIG. 5**). Repeat the thread path several times to reinforce. Secure the working thread and trim. Use the tail thread to repeat this step at the other end of the bracelet, using the other half of the clasp.

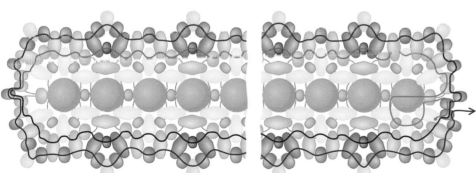

FIG. 4: Completing the Row 3 end through Row 7

MAIN COLORWAY

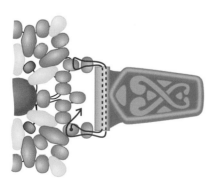

FIG. 5: Adding the clasp

Artist's Tips

- Use any contrasting size 11° or 8° seed bead as a stop bead.

- Cull your two-hole seed beads before you begin, checking that both holes in each are open.

Knot of Hercules

Carole Horn

techniques

Ladder stitch

Tubular herringbone stitch

Square stitch

Flat and tubular peyote stitch

Fringe

materials

1 g silver-lined teal size 15° seed beads (A)

1 g metallic bronze size 15° seed beads (B)

1 g metallic purple size 15° seed beads (C)

1 g light gold luster size 15° charlottes (D)

25 g matte metallic navy iris size 11° seed beads (E)

2 g metallic bronze size 11° cylinder beads (F)

1 aquamarine 12mm crystal rivoli

16 olivine AB 2×4mm crystal bicones

8 tanzanite AB 2×4mm crystal bicones

8 white opal 4×3mm fire-polished rondelles

1 black 7mm snap

Blue and tan size D nylon beading thread

Smoke 6 lb braided beading thread

tools

Scissors

Size 10 and 12 beading needles

finished size

8" (20.5 cm)

1 Knot Loop

Form a herringbone tube for the knot loop:

BASE: Use 4' (1.2 cm) of blue thread to string 4E, leaving a 6" (15 cm) tail. Pass through the 4E again and position the beads so they sit side by side in stacks of 2 beads each. String 2E; pass through the previous 2E and the 2E just added to form a third stack. Continue ladder-stitching 2 beads at a time to form a strip 6 stacks long. Stitch the last stack to the first stack to form a ring. Exit from the first stack (**FIG. 1**).

TUBE: String 2E; pass down through the top E of the next 2E stack along the base and up through the top E of the following stack (**FIG. 2**). Repeat twice for a total of 6E. Step up for the next round through the first E added in this round. Continue working in tubular herringbone stitch until the tube is 3" (7.5 cm) long, stepping up after each round. Your thread will exit a bead in the first stack. *NOTE: Keep the thread tension firm and even as you work.* Secure the tail thread and trim.

JOIN: Bend the tube into a U shape so the ends form 2 side-by-side columns. Position the tube so the stack the thread is exiting is between the 2 columns and the beads in the first stack are next to each other. To connect the columns, square-stitch 2 beads on the first stack of the opposite column to the corresponding 2 beads on the column where the thread is exiting. Exit through the same bead as at the start (**FIG. 3**). Turn the loop over and repeat on the other side of the tube ends, square-stitching the columns together through the adjoining 2 pairs of beads. Exit through the end bead of the second square-stitch connection.

2 Bracelet Band

Form a tubular herringbone-stitch section for the bracelet band:

ROUNDS 1 AND 2: Work 6 tubular herringbone stitches around the joined columns with 2E in each stitch for a total of 12E in each of 2 rounds. Step up through the first bead added in this and subsequent rounds (**FIG. 4, ORANGE THREAD**).

ROUND 3: String 2E; pass down through the next E, string 1E, and pass up through the next E. Repeat for a total of 18E (**FIG. 4, PURPLE THREAD**).

ROUND 4: String 2E; pass down through the next E, string 2E, and pass up through the next E. Repeat for a total of 24E (**FIG. 4, BLUE THREAD**).

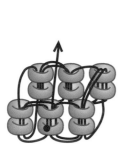

FIG. 1: Ladder-stitching the base

FIG. 2: Starting the herringbone-stitch loop

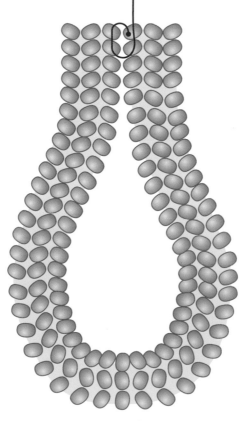

FIG. 3: Joining the loop

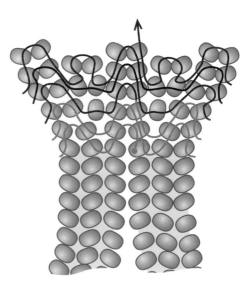

FIG. 4: Increasing the band

ROUND 5: String 2E; pass down through the next E and continue through the next E of Round 4. String 2E; pass through the next E of Round 4 and pass up through the first E on the next stack. Repeat six times, adding a total of 12 herringbone stitches with 2E in each stitch for a total of 24E (**FIG. 4, RED THREAD**).

ROUNDS 6–28: Work a total of 23 rounds with 24E in each round.

ROUND 29: Work 2 stitches with 2E in each stitch and 1 stitch with 1E. Repeat four times for a total of 20E (**FIG. 5, BLUE THREAD**).

ROUNDS 30–35: Work 8 stitches with 2E in each stitch, skipping each 1E added in Round 29, for a total of 6 rounds with 16E in each round (**FIG. 5, RED THREAD**). *NOTE: It is important to use tight tension when working these rounds.*

ROUND 36: Reverse the direction and, without adding another round of beads, stitch up and down through the top beads in each stack to stabilize the edge (**FIG. 6**). Flatten the tube so the folded edges align with the knot loop. Weave through beads and exit a bead at either folded edge.

CLASP LOOP: String 20F; skip 6 beads along the edge and pass down through the next E. Pass up through the E on the next stack and pass back through the last F strung. Work peyote stitch across the loop with 1F in each stitch for a total of 10F. Pass down through the E next to where the loop starts and exit through the E at the loop's start. Peyote-stitch across the loop with 2A in each stitch for a total of 18A (**FIG. 7**). Secure the thread and trim.

Repeat Steps 1 and 2 to form a second bracelet section.

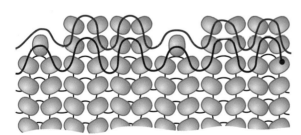

FIG. 5: Decreasing the band

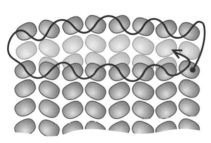

FIG. 6: Stabilizing the edge

MAIN COLORWAY

③ Clasp

Use tubular peyote stitch to bezel a rivoli for the clasp closure, then embellish the bezel with fringe:

ROUNDS 1 AND 2: Use 5' (1.5 m) of braided beading thread to string 32F; knot the tail and working thread to form a ring, leaving a 6" (15 cm) tail. Pass through the first bead added (**FIG. 8, PURPLE THREAD**).

ROUNDS 3 AND 4: Work 1F in each stitch for a total of 16F in each of 2 rounds. Step up through the first bead added in this and subsequent rounds (**FIG. 8, ORANGE THREAD**).

ROUNDS 5 AND 6: Work 1B in each stitch for a total of 16B in each of 2 rounds (**FIG. 8, GREEN THREAD**).

ROUND 7: Work 3 stitches with 1D in each stitch, then work a decrease by weaving through the next B of Round 5 and B of Round 6. Repeat three times for a total of 12D (**FIG. 8, BLUE THREAD**).

ROUND 8: Pass through the next 2D of Round 7 and string 1D. Pass through the next 3D and string 1D; repeat twice for a total of 4D. Pass through the next D

ALTERNATE COLORWAY BACK OF BRACELET

of Round 7 (**FIG. 8, RED THREAD**). Weave through beads to exit 1F of Round 1. Secure the tail thread and trim.

ROUNDS 9 AND 10: Insert the rivoli faceup into the bezel and hold it in place while stitching. Work 1A in each stitch for a total of 16A in each of 2 rounds (**FIG. 9**). Secure the thread, but don't trim. Weave through beads to exit 1F of Round 3.

UPPER FRINGE: String 1 olivine bicone and 4D; pass back through the first D and bicone and pass through the next F of

Round 3 (**FIG. 10**). Repeat for a total of 16 upper fringes. Weave through beads to exit 1F of Round 4.

LOWER FRINGE: String 1 rondelle, 1F, 1 tanzanite bicone, and 1C; pass back through the bicone, 1F, and rondelle, then pass through the next F of Round 4, the nearest F of Round 3, and the next F of Round 4 (**FIG. 11**). Repeat for a total of 8 lower fringes. Secure the thread, but don't trim. Set aside.

FIG. 7: Stitching the clasp loop

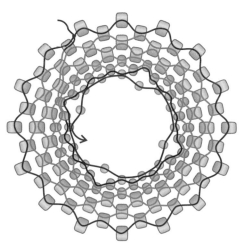

Fig. 8: Working Rounds 1–8 of the bezel

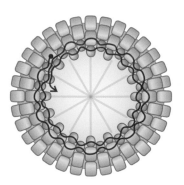

Fig. 9: Securing the rivoli

TAB: Using 3' (0.9 m) of tan thread, peyote-stitch a strip 8F wide and 33 rows long, leaving a 10" (25.5 cm) tail. Work 1 more row with 1B in each stitch. Weave through a few rows of beads and sew one half of the snap to the strip about ¼" (6 mm) from the end (**FIG. 12**). Secure the working thread and trim. Using the tail thread, work 1 row of peyote stitch with B, weave through a few rows of beads, and sew the remaining snap half to the strip about ¼" (6 mm) from the tail end, making sure the snap closes correctly when the strip is wrapped around the clasp loops. Secure the thread and trim.

ATTACH THE RIVOLI: Using the working thread on the rivoli's bezel, sew the rivoli to the center of the peyote strip. Secure the thread and trim.

④ Assembly

Pass 1 clasp loop through 1 knot loop and pass the other clasp loop through the other knot loop (**SEE PHOTOGRAPH BELOW**). Pull the ends away from each other, gently tightening the loops to form the Hercules knot. *NOTE: If desired, start a 1' (0.3 m) length of thread at the end of each knot loop and tack the loop into place on the bracelet band.* Secure the threads and trim. Snap the peyote strip around both clasp loops to fasten the bracelet.

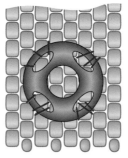

Artist's Tips

- To change the bracelet's length, stitch each bracelet section up to the start of the Round 29 decrease. Connect the two sides to form the Hercules knot and decide how much more (or less) you need to stitch to achieve the correct size. Allow about 1¼" (3.2 cm) on each side (2½" [6.5 cm] total) for the decreases, finishing rounds, and clasp as you make your adjustments.

- Ending with a step-up completes the round and allows you to begin your new thread any place along the tube.

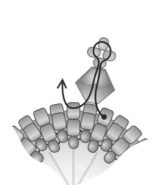

Fig. 10: Forming the top fringe

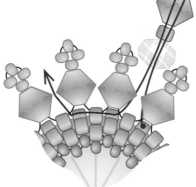

Fig. 11: Stitching the bottom fringe

Fig. 12: Attaching the snap

Lacy Marquise

Norma Jean Dell

techniques

Picot

Netting

materials

2 g metallic light bronze size 15° seed beads (A)

1 g metallic light bronze size 11° seed beads (B)

3 g metallic pink gold size 11° cylinder beads (C)

8 aqua-and-gold 8×17mm pressed-glass flat, pointed ovals (D)

2 brass 4.5mm jump rings

1 brass 17mm toggle clasp

Smoke 6 lb braided beading thread

tools

Scissors

Size 12 beading needle

2 pairs of chain- or flat-nose pliers

finished size

7" (18 cm)

① Component 1

Use picots to encircle and embellish an oval bead:

ROUND 1: Use 3' (0.9 m) of thread to string 1D and 15C; pass through the D, leaving a 6" (15 cm) tail and allowing the C to line one edge of the D. String 15C; pass through the D and position the new C along the other edge of the D (**FIG. 1, BLUE THREAD**). Pass through the first 15C. String 1C; pass through the next 15C. String 1C; pass through the first 4C added in this round (**FIG. 1, RED THREAD**).

ROUND 2: String 3C and pass through the last C exited and the next 4C of Round 1; repeat around the oval seven times for a total of 8 picots. Step up through the first 2C of the first picot added in this round (**FIG. 2**). *NOTE: You will now be working in the opposite direction.*

ROUND 3: *String 4A, 1B, and 3A; pass through the top C of the next picot of Round 2. String 3A, 1B, and 4A; pass through the top C of the following picot. String 2A, 1B, and 2A; pass through the top C of the next picot; repeat.

Repeat from * to connect the rest of the Round 2 picots. Exit from the first B added in this round (**FIG. 3, BLUE THREAD**).

ROUND 4: String 3A; pass through the last B exited and the next 3A and 1C. String 3A; pass through the last C exited and the next 3A and 1B. String 3A; pass through the last B exited and the next 4A and 1C. String 3A; pass through the last C exited and the next 2A, 1B, 2A, and 1C. String 6A (for the clasp loop); pass through the last C exited and the next 2A, 1B, 2A, and 1C. String 3A; pass through the last C exited and the next 4A and 1B. String 3A; pass through the last B exited and the next 3A and 1C. String 3A; pass through the last C exited and the next 3A and 1B. String 3A; pass through the last B exited (**FIG. 3, RED THREAD**). Secure the threads and trim; set aside.

② Component 2

Stitch a second component to connect to the first:

ROUNDS 1 AND 2: Repeat Rounds 1 and 2 of Component 1.

Artist's Tips

- Keep tight tension by wrapping the tail thread around the index finger of your non dominant hand and squeezing it with your middle finger.

- If using different-size ovals, adjust the bead counts in each round and make sure the picots are still evenly spaced.

FIG. 1: Forming Round 1 of the first component

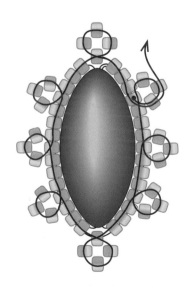

FIG. 2: Stitching the Round 2 picots

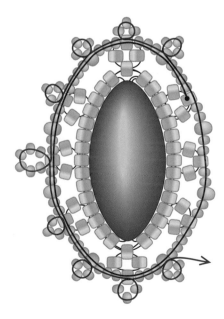

FIG. 3: Adding Rounds 3 and 4 of the first component

ROUND 3: String 4A, 1B, and 3A; pass through the top C in the next picot of Round 2. String 3A, 1B, and 4A; pass through the top C in the following picot. String 2A; pass through the open B at the upper right of the previous component. String 2A; pass through the top C in the next picot of this connector. String 2A; pass through the open B at the lower right of the previous component. String 2A; pass through the top C in the next picot of this connector. String 4A, 1B, and 3A; pass through the top C in the next picot of Round 2. String 3A, 1B, and 4A; pass through the top C in the following picot. String 2A, 1B, and 2A,

then pass through the top C in the next picot; repeat. Exit from the first B added in this round (**FIG. 4, BLUE THREAD**).

ROUND 4: Repeat Round 4 of Component 1, this time only adding the 3A picots to the B/C/B at the top and bottom of this component (**FIG. 4, RED THREAD**). Secure the thread and trim.

③ Components 3–7
Repeat Component 2 five times.

④ Component 8
Repeat Rounds 1–3 of Component 2, then repeat Round 4 of Component 1 to mirror the picots and clasp loop of Component 1.

⑤ Clasp
Use 1 jump ring to connect one half of the clasp to the clasp loop at one end of the bracelet. Repeat at the other end of the bracelet using the other half of the clasp.

FIG. 4: Connecting and finishing the second component

variation

To make earrings, bead one component with picots down the sides and bottom. Add the connector loop at the top and attach an ear wire.

Lasso Loops

Teresa Sullivan

technique

Tubular herringbone stitch

materials

10 g metallic teal 5×3mm 2-hole seed beads (A)

10 g metallic dark copper 5×3mm 2-hole seed beads (B)

10 g metallic light purple 5×3mm 2-hole seed beads (C)

Teal beading thread
(The designer recommends a doubled size A Silamide, size D Nymo, or 6 lb FireLine braided beading thread)

Thread conditioner

tools

Scissors

Size 12 beading needles

Chain-nose pliers (optional)

finished size

7¼" (18.5 cm) (inside circumference)

① Rope

Use tight tension and 2-hole seed beads to form a tubular herringbone–stitch rope:

ROUNDS 1 AND 2: Use 6' (1.8 m) of conditioned thread to string 4A, 4B, and 4C, leaving a 4" (10 cm) tail. Use the working and tail threads to tie a knot, forming a circle. Step up for the next round by passing through the bottom hole of the A nearest the knot and the top hole of the following A (**FIG. 1, BLACK THREAD**).

ROUND 3: String 2A; pass down through the top hole of the next A in the starting circle (**FIG. 1, GREEN THREAD**). Skip the next 1A/1B and pass up through the top hole of the next B in the starting circle. String 2B; pass down through the top hole of the next B in the starting circle (**FIG. 1, BLUE THREAD**). Skip the next 1B/1C and pass up through the top hole of the next C in the starting circle. String 2C; pass down through the top hole of the next C in the starting circle. Skip the next 1C/1A and pass up through the top hole of the second A in the starting circle. Step up through the top hole of the first A added in this round (**FIG. 1, RED THREAD**).

ROUND 4: String 2A; pass down through the top hole of the next A in the previous round and up through the top hole of

the next B in the previous round (**FIG. 2, GREEN THREAD**). String 2B; pass down through the top hole of the next B in the previous round and up through the top hole of the next C in the previous round (**FIG. 2, BLUE THREAD**). String 2C; pass down through the top hole of the next C in the previous round and up through the top hole of the first A in the previous round. Step up through the top hole of the first A added in this round (**FIG. 2, RED THREAD**). *NOTE: Use chain-nose pliers to help guide the needle through the proper holes as needed.*

ROUNDS 5–65: Repeat Round 4 sixty-one times to form a rope about 9" (23 cm) long or until the piece is long enough to fit over your knuckles when it is in a circle.

② Connect

Bend the rope so the first and last rounds meet. Use a herringbone-stitch thread path to weave the rounds together (**FIG. 3**). Secure the thread and trim. *NOTE: Because they're loose at the bottom, the beads of Round 1 tend to spread the wrong way (they won't "toe in" like they should, because they're attached only at the top); it helps to look at Round 2 to see where to pass the needle in and out.*

MAIN COLORWAY

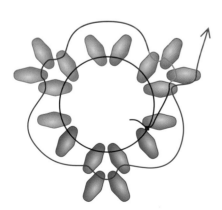

FIG. 1: Forming Rounds 1–3 of the rope

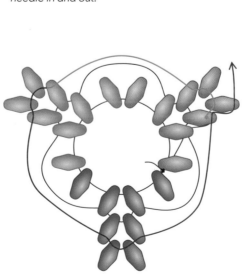

FIG. 2: Stitching Round 4 of the rope

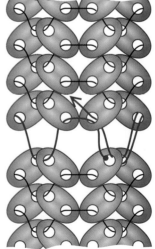

FIG. 3: Joining the rope ends

Tips for Working Tubular Herringbone Stitch with Twin Beads

- Unless you don't mind using a super long length of thread, you'll have to change threads at least once while making the piece. Follow the existing thread path when ending and starting the thread, and use half-hitch knots along the way.

- When stepping up, your needle will naturally want to pass through the bottom hole, but be sure to exit the top hole instead.

- If you want the piece to twist, simply align the beads one column over before joining the rope ends. This works best when using beads all the same color.

- The thread will show on the outside of the step-up beads, so when altering the pattern, choose a thread that matches the beads you'll be stepping up through.

Artist's Tip

- When you end and begin threads, be sure to maintain the same step-up spot. The step-up spot tends to bend the piece inward, which is fine, because you'll need to bend the piece into a circle when joining it into a bangle. However, if the step-up spot changes, this nice curvature will change direction. With this in mind, complete any round before ending your thread, and be careful to maintain that same step-up spot.

ALTERNATE COLORWAYS

Lavender Weave

Shae Wilhite

techniques
Herringbone stitch variation

Rope edging

materials
6 g matte dusty rose size 11° seed beads (A)

20 g pale green Picasso 5×2.5mm 2-hole
   seed beads (B)

1 gold-plated 10×26mm 4-strand slide clasp

Smoke 6 lb braided beading thread

tools
Scissors

Size 10 beading needle

finished size
7⅞" (20 cm)

MAIN COLORWAY

1 Base

Use a variation of flat herringbone stitch to form the bracelet:

ROW 1: Add a stop bead to 6' (1.8 m) of thread, leaving a 6" (15 cm) tail. String {1B and 1A} four times (**FIG. 1, BLUE THREAD**).

ROW 2: String 1B and 1A; pass back through the open (top) hole of the fourth B and the third A of the previous row. String 1B and 1A and pass back through the next B (top hole) and A; repeat. String 1B and 1A; pass back through the top hole of the next B. Step up by passing back through the last A added in this row (**FIG. 1, RED THREAD**).

ROW 3: Repeat Row 2 (**FIG. 2**).

ROWS 4–64: Repeat Row 2 sixty-one times. *NOTE: The B will alternate angles in each row.*

Clasp

*String 3A; pass through the first loop on one half of the clasp and pass back through the last A just added. String 2A; pass through the nearest B (top hole) and A of Row 64. Repeat from * three times to attach the end of the base to the next 3 clasp loops; exit through the end B (top hole) in the final repeat (**FIG. 3, BLUE THREAD**).

3 Rope Edging

String 7A and pass through the bottom hole (toward the beadwork) of the next edge B and then through the top hole (away from the beadwork) of the same edge B, with your needle exiting on top of the loop just formed; repeat thirty times. (**FIG. 3, RED THREAD**). *NOTE: Make sure each new loop lays on top of the previous loop.*

4 Finishing

Weave through beads to exit the end A of Row 1 and repeat Step 2, using the other half of the clasp. *NOTE: Make sure the clasp is positioned so it will close properly.* Repeat Step 3 along the other edge of the base. Remove the stop bead. Secure the threads and trim.

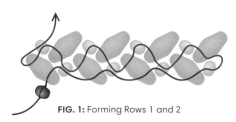

FIG. 1: Forming Rows 1 and 2

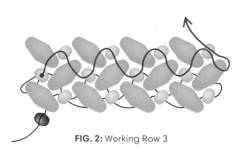

FIG. 2: Working Row 3

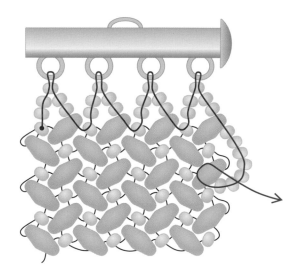

FIG. 3: Attaching the clasp and beading the edge

Artist's Tips

- Not all two-hole seed beads sold as SuperDuos have thinly tapered edges. The rounded or smooth-edged style of SuperDuo or Twin beads looks best in this bracelet. If you can't find them, try substituting Rulla beads. SuperDuos with tapered edges will work, but you'll have more thread show.

- To save time and frustration, check both holes of your two-hole seed beads for blocked holes before you use them.

ALTERNATE COLORWAYS

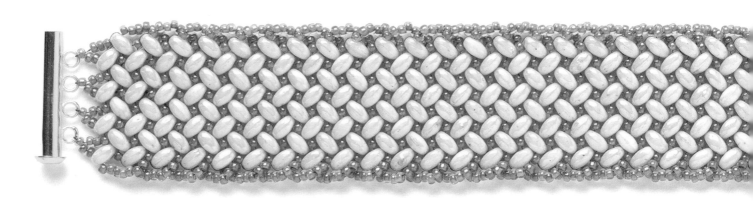

Lilian

Svetlana Chernitsky

techniques

Peyote stitch

Netting

materials

5 g metallic rainbow iris size 11° seed beads (A)

14 g Picasso lavender opaque 5×2.5mm 2-hole seed beads (B)

1 g blue iris 5×2.5mm 2-hole seed beads (C)

3 g smoky topaz transparent 5×3mm 2-hole cylinder beads (D)

5 g metallic bronze 3.4mm Japanese drops (E)

3 antiqued brass 5mm jump rings

1 antiqued brass 16mm flower toggle clasp

Smoke 6 lb braided beading thread

tools

Size 12 beading needle

2 pairs of chain- or flat-nose pliers

finished size

7" (18 cm)

① Body

Work peyote stitch and netting to form the bracelet's body:

ROWS 1 AND 2: Add a stop bead to the end of 6' (1.8 m) of thread, leaving a 12" (30.5 cm) tail. String {1A, 3B, 1A, and 1D} twice. String 1A, 3B, 1A, 1E, and 1A; pass through the second hole of the last B added (**FIG. 1, BLUE THREAD**).

ROW 3: String 1B; skip the next B in the previous row and pass through the second hole of the following B. String 1B and 1A; pass through the second hole of the next D in the previous row. String 1A; skip the next B in the previous row and pass through the second hole of the following B. String 1A; pass through the second hole of the next D in the previous row. String 1A and 1B; pass through the second hole of the next B in the previous row. String 1B; skip the next B in the previous row and pass through the second hole of the following B (**FIG. 1, RED THREAD**).

ROW 4: String 1A, 1E, 1A, and 1B; pass through the second hole of the last B in the previous row. String 1B; pass through the second hole of the next B in the previous row. String 1A, 1D, 1A, 1B, 1A, 1D, and 1A; pass through the second hole of the next B in the previous row. String 1B; pass through the second hole of the next B in the previous row. String 1B, 1A, 1E, and 1A; pass through the second hole of the last B added (**FIG. 2, BLUE THREAD**).

ROW 5: String 1B; pass through the second hole of the next B in the previous row. String 1A; pass through the second hole of the next D in the previous row. String 1A and 1B; pass through the second hole of the next B in the previous row. String 1B and 1A; pass through the second hole of the following D in the previous row. String 1A; pass through the second hole of the next B in the previous row. String 1B; pass through the second hole of the following B in the previous row (**FIG. 2, RED THREAD**).

ROW 6: String 1A, 1E, 1A, and 1B; pass through the second hole of the last B in the previous row. String 1B and 4A; pass through the second hole of the next B in the previous row. String 1C; pass through the next B in the previous row. String 4A and 1B; pass through the second hole of the next B in the previous row. String 1B, 1A, 1E, and 1A; pass through the second hole of the last B added (**FIG. 3**).

ROW 7, LEFT COLUMN: String 1B; pass through the second hole of the next B in the previous row. String 1B and step up through the second hole of the B just added (**FIG. 4, GREEN THREAD**).

ROW 8, LEFT COLUMN: String 1B; pass through the second hole of the next B in the previous row. String 1B, 1A, 1E, and 1A; pass through the second hole of the B just added (**FIG. 4, BLUE THREAD**).

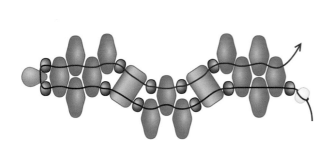

FIG. 1: Forming Rows 1–3

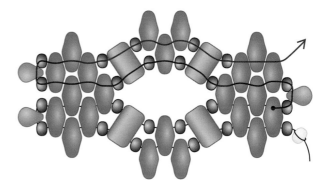

FIG. 2: Adding Rows 4 and 5

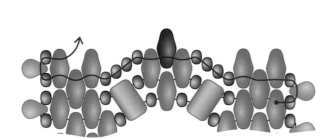

FIG. 3: Stitching Row 6

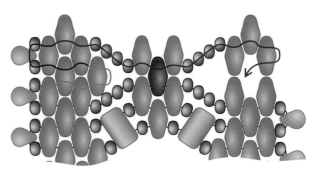

FIG. 4: Adding Rows 7–9, left column, and Rows 8 and 9, right column

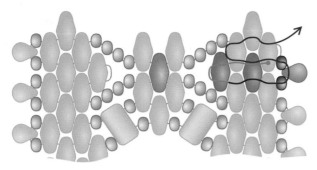

FIG. 5: Forming Row 7, right column

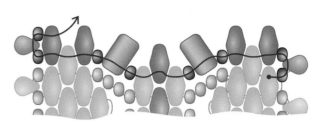

FIG. 6: Stitching Row 10

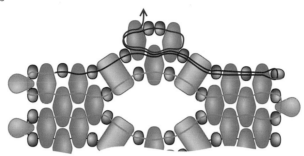

FIG. 7: Adding Rows 43–46

ROW 9, LEFT COLUMN AND ROWS 8 AND 9, RIGHT COLUMN: String 1B; pass through the second hole of the next B in the previous row. String 4A and 1B; pass through the second hole of the nearest C. String 1B, 4A, and 3B; pass through the second hole of the last B added (**FIG. 4, RED THREAD**).

ROW 7, RIGHT COLUMN: String 1B; skip 1B and pass through the second (bottom) hole of the next B in the previous row. String 1B; pass through the second hole of the B just added (**FIG. 5, GREEN THREAD**). Pass through the second (top) hole of the nearest B in Row 6, through the second (bottom) hole of the B previously added, and through the second (top) hole of the next B in Row 6 (**FIG. 5, BLUE THREAD**). String 1A, 1E, and 1A; pass through the bottom hole of the nearest B in Row 8, then weave through beads to exit from the top hole of the same B (**FIG. 5, RED THREAD**).

ROW 10: String 1A, 1E, 1A, and 1B; pass through the second hole of the next B in Row 9. String 1B, 1A, 1D, and 1A; pass through the second hole of the following B in Row 9. String 1B; pass through the second hole of the next B in Row 9. String 1A, 1D, 1A, and 1B; pass through the second hole of the following B in Row 9. String 1B, 1A, 1F, and 1A; pass through the second hole of the last B added (**FIG. 6**).

ROWS 11–42: Repeat Rows 3–10 four times.

ROWS 43 AND 44: Repeat Rows 3 and 4 (**FIG. 7, GREEN THREAD**).

ROW 45: String 1A; pass through the second hole of the next B in the previous row. String 1A; pass through the second hole of the next D in the previous row. String 1A and 1B; pass through the second hole of the next B in the previous row. String 1B and 1A; pass through the second hole of the next D in the previous row. String 1A and pass

through the second hole of the next B in the previous row; repeat. String 1A; pass back through the B just exited and weave through beads to exit from the second hole of the first B added in this row (**FIG. 7, BLUE THREAD**)

ROW 46: String 2A; pass through the second hole of the second B in the previous row, through the bottom hole of that same bead, then weave through beads to exit from the top hole of the first B in the previous row (**FIG. 7, RED THREAD**). Repeat the thread path several times to reinforce; secure the working thread and trim.

Remove the stop bead. Use the tail thread to repeat Row 46 at the other end of the bracelet body.

 Clasp

Use 1 jump ring to connect the clasp ring to Row 46. Use a chain of 2 jump rings to connect the clasp bar to the other end of the bracelet.

Contributors

SANDIE BACHAND

SUE CHARETTE-HOOD
www.crystalwonders.etsy.com
www.originalstexas.com/workshops/

JANICE CHATHAM
bighjh2@aol.com

SVETLANA CHERNITSKY
www.lirigal.com

JANN CHRISTIANSEN
www.dancingseadesigns.etsy.com

ALICE COELHO
www.instagram.com/alsnco/
cacoelhobeads@gmail.com

CSILLA CSIRMAZ
Shilabead
www.shilabead.com
shilabead@gmail.com

MONIQUE DE BOER
www.wirwarkralen.nl
www.etsy.com/shop/WirWarKralen
www.facebook.com/WirwarKralen/
info@wirwarkralen.nl

NORMA JEAN DELL
www.njdesigns1.com

PENNY DIXON
www.pennydixondesigns.com

BARBARA FALKOWITZ
info@artfulbeadstudio.com

LESLEE FRUMIN
www.lesleefrumin.om
www.instagram.com/lesleefrumin/
esfrumin@mac.com

JULIE GLASSER
www.julieglasser.com
www.etsy.com/shop/JulRiDesign
www.instagram.com/julridesign/
jglasserdesigns@gmail.com

MICHELLE GOWLAND
therollingbeadweaver.com
www.facebook.com/rolling.beadweaver.3
www.instagram.com/
the_rolling_beadweaver_/
therollingbeadweaver@gmail.com

SMADAR GROSSMAN
www.etsy.com/shop/SmadarsTreasure
smadarstreasure@gmail.com

AMY HAFTKOWYCZ
www.etsy.com/shop/TrixiesJewelBox
www.instagram.com/trixiesjewelbox/
TrixiesJewelBox@gmail.com

CAROLE E. HANLEY

CAROLE HORN
carolehorn@nyc.rr.com

GAIL MCLAIN
www.facebook.com/harborartgallery/
sgmclain@olypen.com

MARIA TERESA MORAN
www.facebook.com/Maria-Teresa-
Moran-1020679601305809/

CHRISTINA NEIT
www.goodquillhunting.com
christina@goodquillhunting.com

CAROLE OHL
Bead Stash: Dayton, Ohio
www.etsy.com/shop/openseed
caroleohl@gmail.com

JANET PALUMBO
www.2BeadsRBetterThan1.etsy.com
www.facebook.com/2BRBT1
www.instagram.com/2beadsr1/
2BeadsR1@gmail.com

CARMELLA PATZLAFF
patzlaff@sbcglobal.net

GLENDA PAUNONEN
www.beadsgonewild.com

REGINA PAYNE
www.nightowlstudiojewels.etsy.com

CRISTIE PRINCE
www.glassyjewels.com
cristie@glassyjewels.com

ROXI ROGERS
roxi.rogers@aol.com

YASMIN SARFATI
www.beadingwithbeads.net

MARJORIE SCHWARTZ
bschwar13@msn.com

JENNIFER SCHWARTZENBERGER
www.etsy.com/people/StonyCreekBead

SUSAN G. SCHWARTZENBERGER
www.etsy.com/people/StonyCreekBead

KASSIE SHAW
www.beadingbutterfly.com
beadingbutterflyshop.etsy.com
kassie@beadingbutterfly.com

SUSAN SEVERS COUNCIL
www.bead-therapy.com
www.facebook.com/beadtherapy1
susan@bead-therapy.com

RACHEL SIM
simraq@gmail.com

NICHOLE STARMAN
www.NicholeStarman.etsy.com

TERESA SULLIVAN
www.teresasullivanstudio.com
www.teresasullivanstudio.etsy.com

HORTENSE E. THOMPSON
www.beadybeadz.com

LIISA TURUNEN
www.liisaturunendesigns.com

SHAE WILHITE
www.sweetbeadslv.com/

JILL WISEMAN
jillwisemandesigns.com
jill@jillwisemandesigns.com

SÁRA ZSADON
www.beademecum.hu

METRIC CONVERSION CHART		
TO CONVERT	**TO**	**MULTIPLY BY**
Inches	Centimeters	2.54
Centimeters	Inches	0.4
Feet	Centimeters	30.5
Centimeters	Feet	0.03
Yards	Meters	0.9
Meters	Yards	1.1

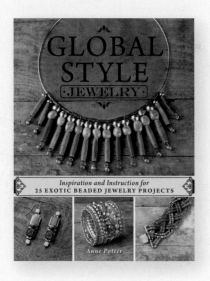
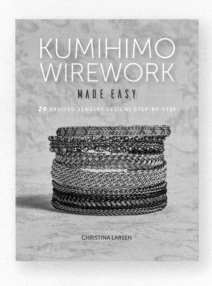